Primary Femininity

Discussions on a Central Identity

Edited by
M. Sagman
Kayatekin

Primary Femininity

Discussions on a Central Identity

Edited by M. Sagman Kayatekin

IPBOOKS.net

International Psychoanalytic Books (IPBooks)
New York • www.IPBooks.net

International Psychoanalytic Books (IPBooks), Queens, NY

Online at: www.IPBooks.net

Cover painting: Electra at the Tomb of Agamemnon,
1869 by Frederic Leighton

Cover and interior book design by Kathy Kovacic, Blackthorn Studio

ISBN: 978-1-969031-12-0

Primary Femininity
Discussions on a Central Identity

Edited by M. Sagman Kayatekin

From the Desk of the Editor

M. Sagman Kayatekin

This book has two sections.

The first and the main section is on Arlene Richards's scholarly and evocative lead paper. As expected, her ideas kindled a vigorous, creative set of controversies, conversations with the contributors of this volume. I have a conversation with Arlene Richards that gives an individual, historical narrative of a period of her life, with the hope that it provides a relevant sketch of the uniquely personal context of her creative inquiries and thinking in psychoanalysis.

The second section, that is titled as "history," in fact is quite relevant for our current day, as Ellman's paper and Galdi's dialogue with it suggests. The minutiae of the early history of psychoanalysis are fascinating, as a serious topic in itself, and as a microcosm of how creative ideas, schools of thought develop.

I hope our readers will find the book enjoyably thought provoking.

With my deep respect to our readers,
M. Sagman Kayatekin, M.D.

The Female Oedipus Complex

Arlene Kramer Richards, EdD

The conversation about the Oedipus Complex in girls has been controversial and complicated, knotty and sometimes even vitriolic. Beginning with Freud's early ideas about penis envy as bedrock and suppression of the clitoris as ideal adulthood and coming to present day emphasis on relationships, variability and individuality, passion on this topic has run high. A kind of watershed appeared as early as the International Psychoanalytic conference in Marienbad in 1936 when Karen Horney presented a paper contradicting Freud's ideas and, in turn, was highly criticized by Freud. Despite Freud's plea for female psychoanalysts to enlighten him and their colleagues about female sexuality, he summarily rejected Horney's contentions that a girl's relationship with her mother was formative and that the father was less important in her view of herself and her world. A second watershed was Applegarth's (1977) review of a book by Nagera called *Female Sexuality and the Oedipus Complex*. Applegarth noted Nagera's reliance on the ideas of castration and penis envy to understand female development and posited the importance of relationships with the parents. In this, she was following Horney and leading a new parade of analytic thinkers.

By 1998 Hopwood responded to Halberstadt-Freud's contention that the female developmental story needed to include a place for aggression and resolution of hatred of the mother as exemplified in the Electra story. Hopwood compared Halberstadt-Freud's view with that of Kulish and Holtzman (1998).The latter authors proposed the Persephone myth as a model for female development. As will be clear later, these other myths have never attained to acceptance for female development that Oedipus has long had as a model for male development. And the consideration of the female development has led to a re-thinking of the male version as well (Munder-Ross 1992).

Lauffer (1986) reconsidered the idea that the female psychosexual development results from a girl's disappointment in her mother for not having provided her daughter with a penis. Lauffer posited a female phase of awareness of her body as a receptacle as a developmental step toward accepting adult femininity and heterosexual desire and pleasure.

My own work on female psychosexual development (1990, 1996, 2003) has had some implications for the understanding of the female Oedipal story. If a little girl experiences pleasure in her own genital, it follows that she will want genital stimulation. Wanting that stimulation from others is the next step in development. Experiencing gratification as love and longing for it gets expressed as wanting to grow up and marry Daddy. Many girls want that; and some want to marry Mommy.

In her recounting of Freud's Oedipal theory for college students, Blass (2001) differentiates between an Oedipal theory based on castration fears and one based on conflictual love-hate for the father. She bases her theory on an earlier paper (Blass 1992) that focuses on the Dora case (Freud, S, 1906).

In that earlier paper Blass makes the case that Freud actually came to the idea that Oedipal wishes were the best explanation of a girl towards her father are the core of neurosis.

Blass puts it this way:

> With his insight that the origin of neurosis is not necessarily associated with an actual event of seduction, Freud sought to assign the girl personal responsibility for her fantasies and actions. Her intra-psychic fantasy, supplied by her fixated infantile drives, fixated as a result of her perverse sexual desires, lay at the foundation of her neurosis. It is interesting that in ascribing responsibility to the patient, Freud not only facilitates the transition to his later oedipal formulations but also inhibits it. The focus on the girl's responsibility was intimately tied to the complete absolution of the father (p. 180).

Blass then contends that all the later theorists who asserted that Freud had a complete Oedipal interpretation of Dora's neurosis were wrong in that Freud actually interpreted the transference not as a transference from father to Freud, but from Herr K., a later seducer to Freud. She seems to insist on ignoring or refuting what the other readers of the case have inferred: the transference from Herr K. was based on a transference from father to Herr K.

Is it possible that the other readers had an understanding of the complexity of transference, a multi-step process with possible iterations? Or that Freud understood things that way?

In her later paper on the teaching of the Oedipal complex Blass makes the point that:

> In the face of the emerging sexual love for the father, the mother becomes a hated rival and yet a beloved one. Since love for the father entails betrayal of the mother it cannot be completely attained and in its place internalization occurs (p. 1112).

Following the complex conversation about the place of the Oedipal conflict in establishing femininity (Maguire, M. & Dewing, H., 2007) asserts that:

> Marie: The idea of a (heterosexual) parental couple and a split between identification and desire is intrinsic to oedipal theories. The girl is expected to desire her father and become like her mother. Heterosexual 'femininity' and 'masculinity' are seen as the more 'secure' and 'mature' identities, though. many patients do not identify themselves—or their parents—in this way (p. 532).

> But this complication has clinical implications for treating women who do not conform to this pattern as less "normal" than those who conform to it. And theory to include other patterns of development. And what could those be?

Buchberg (2014) regards the development of femininity as the outcome of a turn away from the mother and thus toward the father as a melancholia or pathological mourning. Thus, this underlines Freud's idea that what starts a separation process results in dissatisfaction with the female body and results in a sense of castration. The damaged object relation fuels a damaged self-image. In her words:

> Following the course of pathological mourning, the refusal and loss of the girl's mother is preserved in a melancholic structure—the residue of her grudge and her renounced love—and her femininity is thereby founded on a search, which Freud calls penis envy, for an irretrievable past. The damaged object relation is thus the inscription on the headstone of this internal burial site, and an imagined body defect both marks the loss as well as designates the path to its imagined repair (p 129).

But Freud's idea was that a girl's fantasy loss of the penis (which he confounded with castration) was the cause of her turning away from mother and toward father, while Buchberg contends that turning away from mother was the cause of disappointment with her own self and turning to father. In other words, where Freud saw disappointment with anatomy as the cause of change in love object, Buchberg proposes that that loss of the original love object causes disappointment with the anatomy.

Buchberg does not mention a precursor and source of support for her argument in a paper by Kulish & Holtzman (1998) in which they posit an alternative to the idea of the Oedipal constellation in a girl. They conclude that a girl's path to femininity is through her difficulty in separating from her mother; they think Electra is not the model for female development: Persephone is that model. They argue that Persephone's separation from her mother when she falls into Hades is the cause of her sadness and loss of her mother the cause of her becoming prisoner to Hades. Her anger and fear at this loss of her love object make her an involuntary wife, a woman forced to accept a man as a substitute for her mother. In this scenario a girl becomes a woman by being harmed. But the Persephone story has her biting into a pomegranate and staying in Hades for as many months as she had seeds in her mouth. She has six seeds. But she could have taken a tiny bite with no seeds or at less than six. Her part in the story is choosing a big bite and a life spent half with her mother, half with her husband. In the story her husband is her father's brother. That suggests that her choice included both/and rather than either/or. I believe that this implies that a woman integrates ties to her mother as well as her father and wants closeness with both as well as identifications with both.

Camden (2011) argued against the idea of regarding this myth as a template for normal female development. In her view, rape is not the normal introduction to adult sexuality. Nor is the observation that some women seem to reconcile themselves to being raped as Persephone seems to have eventually done in the myth to be taken as making this an acceptable part of normal female development. Thus, the substitution of this myth for an inversion of the Oedipal myth has not gained traction in current psychoanalytic thought, yet object relations theory has.

The many variations on the Persephone myth used by different analytic writers suggest that the story is neither simple nor parallel to the male Oedipus story. Does culture influence what myths are important in a person's view of their world? Does development after the age of six years determine what the wishes and fears are that a child brings into their life as an adolescent and an adult? These questions are answered differently by different analytic theorists. Object relations theorists point to the earlier stages of development as laying down the primary personality and character traits of the person. Theorists who place more importance on cultural influences emphasize later events and relationships in a person's life.

Could current ideas about how traumas in adulthood affect mental life give therapists a better way to understand what can go wrong in development and cause emotional pain and discontent?

Haute (2005) sees the Oedipal and castration complexes in a historical context:

> …problems to which every human child has to give an answer: the inevitable disillusionment of the primary object-love and the confrontation with adult sexuality. I will interpret the Oedipus and castration complexes as a historical as well as a contingent answer to these two problems. In this way, they become much more dependent on culture than Freud could ever admit (p. 1662).

In Buchberg's view a girl repeats her ambivalent attachment to her mother in her relationships with female friends. In Lena Dunham's very popular TV series "Girls" Buchberg notes the opening scene of two female bodies entwined naked and indistinguishable from each other. As the series progresses, they separate, become involved with men, make love, and progress toward maturity. Buchberg, uses a similar but more nuanced idea, that of the melancholy separation in which the loss of the mother is complicated by hostile feelings accompanying love for the mother. This is the female trajectory: Persephone willingly going down into Hades to get away from her mother while also mourning losing her. In essence, Buchberg uses Butler's (1990) idea of femininity based on incomplete mourning for the girl's loss of her mother as a sexual love object.

Still wrestling with the idea of a female version of the Oedipus story Zepf and Seel (2016) come to this conclusion:

> The forms of processing the positive and negative Oedipus complex show that these forms do not end in efforts that are mutually exclusive and that neither wards off the other. Both occur simultaneously and both are warded off. The heterosexual as well as the homosexual shape of the drama are not enacted with the original object in later life, but with its substitutes (p. 415).

They seem to be saying that what have been called the positive and negative forms of the Oedipus complex are really both forms of the triadic situation. This implies that they are understandable without the use of erroneous suppositions about vaginal awareness, awareness of the father's penis, or fantasy of a mother who could only be sexually satisfied by the father's penis. This conclusion seems to me to both simplify and support the idea that the little girl like the little boy wants to be the best beloved of both parents and struggles with the awareness that the parents sleep with each other and exclude her from their nighttime pleasures (p. 416).

All of this hypothesizes a degree of fantasizing and sophistication of logic characteristic of a psychoanalyst, but I submit, not of an infant, toddler, or even a three- to six-year-old child. The cognitive capacity demonstrated by this tour de force of reasoning is beyond that of adolescence, even in the most brilliant child. Attributing such mental gyrations to a young child is not supported by any evidence I know of.

I think the point of so many variants of the female Oedipal myth is that clinical work as well as personal experience cannot be reduced to one story. All of the attempts to understand it get to some of the truth, but individual differences account for so much of observation that any single underlying story is always inadequate to explain female development. At the same time, it is useful to recognize that a person who recognizes herself as female has something important in common with others who recognize themselves as female. That said, it seems to me that compromising between the Oedipal story and the Persephone myth, the story of female development is different from the male because the first love object for a girl is her mother or mothering person, while the father or non-mothering person comes second. Unwilling to give up her mother, a girl wishes for both mother and non-mother to love her best. For a boy, the father is more of an intruder on his exclusive relationship with his mother. Thinking of it in this way, the more usual pattern for a girl is to want to retain her mother's love at the same time as she acquires that of her father. The Oedipal story fits a male identified person so that a boy has a different agenda: that of keeping mother all to himself. The Persephone story understood in in terms of negotiating a triadic situation by spending half the year with mother and the other half with a husband provides a way of understanding female development in general.

The following clinical examples provide evidence for this formulation. A clinical example of the female Oedipus was recently presented to me by a patient from California whom I will call Y. Her daughter had a third birthday party where she insisted on being fed her birthday cake by the patient's husband who was her daughter's father. Y became very angry with her husband who she accused of being stupid in encouraging the child's regression to infantile behavior. This woman hated her own mother for being bossy and for being loyal to her own family of origin rather than to Y and her father.

I thought that her daughter's entry into an Oedipal love affair with her father reawakened her own feelings for her father. Those feelings had been especially intense earlier in the treatment when she had strong feelings of contempt for her husband and fantasies of being with an older, more experienced man. Those feelings and fantasies had abated somewhat after interpretation of her wish to seduce my husband and humiliate me. But that led to intense rejection of her father and resentment of what she recalled as his seductive treatment of her when she was a child.

Together, Y and I reconstructed a scenario in which she and her father had blamed her mother for her devotion to her family of origin. I suggested that she might have resented her mother for not loving her best in all the world. I thought she loved her daughter best and that she could resent her daughter loving her father more than she loved her mother. This exacerbated her resentment of her mother. It was especially painful because Y had no family of origin to protect her.

I thought but did not say that she was in the position of the boy who murdered both of his parents and pleaded for mercy because he was an orphan. Her resentment of both parents left her an emotional orphan. In her mind only her daughter could love her. She could not believe that her husband could love her best in all the world if he too loved their daughter more than anyone in the world.

In the strongly Oedipal situation, with her old longings reawakened by the sight of her daughter's longings, she was able to recognize her hatred of her mother as a reflection of her mother's envy of her and her envy of her mother. She allowed herself to know how powerful she is and to see how she had structured her own life to repair the loss her mother's exclusive love and necessary rejection of her father's intrusive love.

All of this had to do with the triadic situation and the wish to be both mother's and father's best beloved. It suggested to me that the Oedipal situation was a developmental step necessary for both boys and girls. Contrary to the view that a girl blamed her mother for not giving her a penis, it suggested that a girl would blame her mother for not loving her exclusively and eventually blame her father for the same thing. And now, writing about this recalled to me the great pleasure I had felt as a little girl when walking between my parents, one hand clasping my mother's hand, the other clasping my father's. In that moment I could fantasize being both of their best beloved.

Do we need a Greek myth to embody this fantasy? If we take seriously the idea that the Oedipal story is one of revenge against Oedipus' father for having seduced a little boy long before Oedipus was born and for having lamed and exposed Oedipus to death as an infant, we can see that the intergenerational transmission of trauma is the core of the story. Then the wish every child has for being the best beloved of both parents, a wish that had to be frustrated for normal development to take place, is transmitted and frustrated in every generation especially by the most loving of parents.

Another variant of Oedipal imagery and conflict comes from a young woman, who I will call Jane, who believed that she was too ugly to be a girl. She recalled being told by her mother that she as less beautiful than her sister, less beautiful than any of the girls in her class in school, less beautiful than her mother had been as a girl. Although she looked fine to me and to her husband, she dressed drably, wore no makeup or jewelry, and seemed to avoid being noticed. When she wondered why her mother had compared her to others so often and so disparagingly, I suggested that she herself might have been afraid of being too attractive, especially to her loving but distant father she cried.

Over time we constructed a version of her story of a domineering but reliable and caring mother. Jane recalled that her mother had told her that their larger family had been disappointed with Jane for being born a girl and rejected her mother for giving birth to a girl. Jane understood this to mean that she and her mother were the only sources of love for each other. As she understood it, her father was too weak to defend them against the rejection of the big family and too undependable to be trusted. She felt safer not being close to joining her mother as an ally against him. By being unattractive she could defend herself against her wish to be close to him.

Yet another woman, Sara, suffered from compulsive shopping and hoarding. She recognized that she hated her mother's hoarding old clothes and household utensils even to the point that she had filled her bedroom with so much stuff that she had to sleep on a bench in the kitchen of her two-room apartment. Yet she only saw her own hoarding as sensible. The things she wasn't using in the present might come in handy someday. Fashions changed so that what was out of style now could come back next year, or the year after that. She would be ready, on trend. As we worked together, she saw that her identification with her mother was stronger than her distaste for clutter and the fear that she could lose her mother to insanity was impelling her need to keep what she could of both feminine clothes and provisions for the future.

Sara expressed awe of her distant but very successful father. Accepting her father's distance, yet longing to be closer to him, she became an academic with very high standards for herself. She married late, chose a husband who was less educated than she was and less successful at his job. She struggled with resentment at her husband for not being as successful as she or her father was. In the course of analysis, she realized that she had identified with her father and married someone more like her mother. Her mother was a nurturing but fearful and uneducated woman. Sara's identification with her centered on her hoarding. The hoarding was a defense for her mother. It was a response to her fear of the poverty she had experienced as a child. But for Sara it was a way of defending herself against fear of the loss of

13

her femininity. Identifying with her father made her femininity problematic. Understanding this gave her the courage to
clean out her closet of old, outmoded clothes. She ultimately
ended her analysis with a gift to her analyst of a beautiful
blouse.

Sara's analytic journey illustrates her ultimate gain in understanding herself. By untangling the complications of her
attachments to each of her parents, and her identifications
with them, analyst and analysand were able to allow her to
accept a compromise that allowed her to be a more loving
wife, a freer person, and a woman with both self-esteem and
the capacity for nurturing others. I think her analytic journey
shows a courageous and intelligent adaptation to a very painful triangular situation.

In another example of the variants of a girl's development
in the time when she discovers and experiences the intensity
of love for someone other than her primary caretaker, the
time Freud called the Oedipal stage of development, Martine
experienced an abandonment when her parents took a trip to
another country to explore the possibility of immigrating to
that place. Left alone with a nanny she had never met before
the day they left, Martine shut down. She stopped playing
with her toys, refused to go to nursery school, and refused
playdates with her buddies. Although she gradually softened
her attitude toward her nanny, she retained her resentment
toward her mother whom she believed had wanted the trip as
a respite from taking care of her.

By the time I met her as an adult, she had established a part-
time career. She had married and had a child of her own. But
she was very discontent with both her career and her marriage. She believed that her child loved his father more than
he loved her. She also believed that her colleagues at work
liked each other more than they liked her. And she believed
that her husband loved his family of origin more than he loved
her. She saw herself as an unlikeable person. She did all she
could to make me dislike her, demanding constant changes in

schedule, paying late, refusing to accept my way of focusing on her feelings by constantly asking questions about my life, my thoughts, my feelings.

All of this replicated the way she alienated her parents, siblings, colleagues, and even her customers. But it was especially evident in the way she treated her mother. While she identified with her mother's secret extravagances, she also bitterly scorned her as wasteful. And while she regarded her mother's power over Martine's father, she also resented any move her husband made without her permission. She put down his tennis playing yet indulged in her own hobbies. She hated the same traits she identified with, then hated herself for them.

Repeated suggestions that she longed for her father to love her as much as her mother believed that her father had adored and indulged her seemed to her to be attacks rather than attempts at understanding. Her point was that she had really been treated contemptuously by her father. When I finally understood that her need was to have her own reality confirmed, she had taught me something that I have used in my own work ever since. Once that was established, she became more able to tolerate seeing her understanding as only one way of way of understanding, one distorting way of seeing an "objective" reality, one way of blaming her father for her misery rather than recognizing it as distorted by her wish to be his best beloved. The reality was that she was not and never could be more loved by her father in the way that her mother was loved by him. And that was too painful for her to accept. It caused her pain. She tried to alleviate the pain by blaming him, but eventually she could see that the incest taboo was not his invention.

I hope that these examples lead clearly to the suggestion that individual experience of what has been called the Oedipal conflict is determined partly by the universal experience of attachment to the early nurturer, partly by the infant's genetic endowment, partly by parental characteristics, partly by parental fantasies of the child, personality, and partly by the cultural expectations and restrictions that the child is born into.

While all analytic theorists agree on the importance of early childhood in shaping a woman's adult life, some lean more heavily toward emphasizing early infantile attachment, some toward emphasizing toddler phase separation, some toward prioritizing the triangulation of the young child's love and hate, and some toward the centrality of self-esteem, and some point to the disruptive and reorganizing effect of trauma. Recent attempts at integrating some or all of these points of view by Wallerstein (1990)), Rangell (1996), and Pine (2006) have widened the range of understanding of what happens in the analytic situation and what happens in the course of human development.

The main story line in psychoanalysis has been the Oedipal story, mostly derived from Freud's original understanding of the hysterical women he analyzed early in his career and for-mulated again as a result of his self-analysis. Since then, the Oedipal story has been expanded, supplemented by infant observation, attention to issues of self-esteem and self-cohe-sion, and focus on the immediate situation of two people in a room having a conversation that focuses on their interaction and how it meshes with the story of one person's past. This gradual change has led to different schools of psychoanalysis with very different theoretical explanations for mental illness and for theories of cure. All of this has led to a search for a psychoanalytic theory that unifies the diverse theories.

Wallerstein (1990) brought together psychoanalysts from three continents to discuss how their theories affected their analytic understanding and their analytic work. He was attempting to unify theory despite cultural differences. The theorists discussing the issue of the female Oedipus have understood the concept differently in response to cultural changes over time. Both have paid attention to feelings.

Rangell (1996) emphasized the importance of the analyst's experience in shaping the theory he used in analytic work. He could have, but did not explicitly, cite the case of Kohut (1979) who used his own experience of narcissistic injury to formulate a theory of cure based on the analyst's empathic stance. Or the example of Melanie Klein (Grosskurth, 1979) who found it impossibly difficult to tolerate her own children as babies and formulated a theory of pathogenesis in the aggressive impulse of the infant.

For Pine (2006) the idea of a unified theory of psychoanalysis maybe unattainable and unnecessary. He rejects specifically a main story line that could unify developmental, conflictual, relational, narcissistic and similar theories. He contends:

> Clinicians often simply collect it, because they find it useful to do so, never knowing when this or that piece may rise out of their preconscious to clarify a clinical moment. These multitudes of clinical and conceptual bits will all be viewed here as part of a psychoanalytic "dictionary." Given the uncertainties and variations in psychoanalytic clinical work, the dictionary view is often more fruitful than a view of our massive collection of observed and theorized bits as pieces of a novel, even a complex novel, with a known, main explanatory story line (i.e., a general theory) (p. 465).

Pine agrees with and extends Waelder's idea of a unifying theory thus:

> I agreed that every psychic act can indeed be viewed as an attempted "solution" to problems besetting us from the standpoint of the drives, the superego, and external reality, as in Waelder's formulation. But in a modification of his formulation, I proposed that every psychic act can be viewed as an attempted 'solution' (in his phrase) to the compulsion to repeat and argued that this most clearly refers specifically to the repetition of internalized object relationships" (Pine 1990, pp. 480–482).

"And finally, in an addition to Waelder's formulation, I suggested that every psychic act can also be viewed as an attempted solution to problems regarding several forms of disturbance in self-state. Diversity is thus readily incorporated into his scheme (p. 485–486).

Diversity is also essential to the view of treatment as an accumulation of experience on the part of the patient just as much as an accumulation of experience on the part of the analyst or therapist. Just as each therapist has her own accumulation of experience, so each patient does as well. Therefore, each pair has multiple sets of ways to view the past and anticipate the future and the combination is unique. That is why it is not useful to view a patient as "a man" or "a woman". What is interesting and useful, in my experience, is to see the uniqueness in each patient rather than see the person as an example of a class. This applies to the therapist as well. It serves the therapist well to remember that our own experience is unique and therefore limited. The interesting part of our work is the addition to our own experience that comes with each patient and modifies our view of the world inasmuch as we can empathize with what we hear from the patient and how what we hear modifies our own feelings as well as our cognitive understanding.

In this regard we can, if we are open to it, see the possibilities for the patient to solve her problems by reaching her own unique compromise formations. Similarly, we construct our own solutions, our own compromises, out of our previous experiences in life and in treatment and, most importantly, the immediate experiences with the particular patient. A therapist who was herself a patient, once told me, "I like free stroke, not synchronized swimming." She was talking of the pleasure she got from using her unique experience to fashion a therapy that responded to her own immediate problems and those of her patient.

If each patient has her own history, her own understanding of that history, and her own experience of the therapist's or analyst's reactions to what she says and does, then the story of that therapeutic narrative will be engrossing to the therapist and enlightening to the patient. Analytic work of this kind never becomes too confusing for the novice analyst and never goes stale for the experienced analyst. As Fenichel (1941) put it, all one has to do in analysis is listen to the patient's feelings, talk about the patient's feelings, and try to reach a mutual understanding of those feelings. Cognitively simple, but emotionally demanding, this way of treatment is reached independently of the theory the therapist has learned from classes and books. When we treat women, we see them not in contrast to men or other women, we do effective treatment when we allow the patient to become a problem solver rather than a student who learns from us.

Working this way we can answer Wallerstein's conundrum in "One Psychoanalysis or Many?" (1988). Psychoanalysis becomes one in that all psychoanalysts focus on the patient's feelings, and many in that the stories of patients' lives are unique. Psychoanalysis becomes one and myriad. Because it is one, it can be learned and taught, because it is many, it can be useful in different cultures and for the many varieties of sexuality and ways of living as they evolve in the world around us. The way we understand women changes as the culture that shapes us changes so that over space and over time, different theories seem to fit our patient's needs. But the basic idea of paying attention to feelings remains the same. And that attention, both cognitive and emotional, is the power of psychoanalysis.

Pragmatic theory uses patient satisfaction as criterion of truth. What of resistance as a bar to satisfaction? As long as we cannot be sure of a philosophic criterion for science or scientific truth, we are committed to a reliance on process rather than outcome, and relevance rather than predictability, as an assurance of understanding. Is the theoretical concept relevant to the patient's present view of her history? Is she satisfied that she has been understood? Does she feel confident that continuing the process will be useful for her?

These questions point to the individual as criterion of truth. In plainer words: Does it make sense to her? Does it fit her story? Does it address her pain? I think this is what Pine meant when he advocated using whatever theoretical concepts fit the particular patient at the particular moment.

References

Applegarth, A. (1977). Review of *Female Sexuality and the Oedipus Complex* by Humberto Nagera. New York: Jason Aronson, Inc., 1975. 143 pp. *Psychoanal. Q.,* (46):693–695.

Blass, R. (1992). *Did Dora have an Oedipus complex?* PSSC. New Haven: Yale.

——— (2001). The Teaching of the Oedipus Complex: On Making Freud Meaningful to University Students by Unveiling His Essential Ideas on The Human Condition. *International Journal of Psychoanalysis* 82:1105-1121.

Buchberg, L. (2014). Oedipus in Brooklyn: Reading Freud on Women, Watching Lena Dunham's Girls *Psychoanal. Q.,* 83(1):121–150.

Butler, J. (1990). *Gender Trouble.* London: Routledge.

Camden, V. (2011). Review of *A Story of Her Own: The Female Oedipus Complex Re-examined and Renamed.* Nancy Kulish & Deanna Holtzman *American Imago* 68(1):139–148.

Fenichel, O. (1938). Problems of Psychoanalytic Technique. *Psychoanalytic Quarterly* 7:421–442.

Grosskurth, P. (1986). *Melanie Klein: Her World and Her Work.* New York: Knopf.

Haute, R. (2005). Infantile sexuality, primary object love and the anthropological significance of the Oedipus Complex. *Int. J. Psychoanal.,* 86(6):1661–1678.

Holtzman, D. & Kulish, N. (2000). The femininization of the female oedipal complex, part 1: a reconsideration of the significance of separation issues. *J. Amer. Psychoanal. Assn.*, 48:1413–1437.

Hopwood, A. (1999). Halberstadt-Freud, H. C. 'Electra versus Oedipus—Femininity reconsidered', *Int. J. Psycho-Anal.*, 1998, 79, pp. 41—56. Kulish, Nancy & Holtzman, Deanna. 'Persephone, the loss of virginity and the female Oedipus complex', *Int. J. Psycho-Anal.*, 1998, 79, pp. 57–71. *Journal of Analytical Psychology.*, 44:416–417.

Kohut, H. (1979). The Two Analyses of Mr Z. *Int. J. Psychoanal.*, 60:3–27.

Kulish, N. & Holtzman, D. (1998). Persephone, the loss of virginity and the female oedipal complex. *Int. J. Psychoanal.*, 79:57–71.

Laufer, M. (1986). The Female Oedipus Complex and the relationship to the body. *Psychoanalysis. Stud. Child,*. 41: 259–276.

Munder-Ross, J. (1992). *The Male Paradox.* New York: Simon & Schuster.

Pine, F. (2006). The Psychoanalytic Dictionary: A Position Paper on Diversity and its Unifiers. *J. Amer. Psychoanal. Assn.*, 54(2):463–491.

Rangell, L. (1996). The "analytic "in psychoanalytic treatment: how analysis works. *Psych. Inq.* 16:140–166.

Richards, A.K. (1990). Female fetishes and female perversions: "A case of female foot or more properly boot fetishism" by Hermine Hug-Hellmuth reconsidered. *The Psychoanalytic Review* 77:11–23.

———— (1996). Primary femininity and female genital anxiety. *Journal of the American Psychoanalytic Association* 44 (suppl): 261–283.

––––––– (2003) A Fresh Look at Perversion *Journal of the American Psychoanalytic Association* 25(1):1199-1218

Wallerstein, R.S. (1988). One psychoanalysis or many? *Int. J. Psycho-Anal.,* 69: 5-21.

––––––– (1990). Psychoanalysis: The common ground. *Int. J. Psycho-Anal,.* 71:3–20.

Zepf, S. & Seel, D. (2016). Penis Envy and the Female Oedipus Complex a Plea to Reawaken an Ineffectual Debate. *Psychoanal. Rev.,* 103(3):397–421.

Metaphorizing the Oedipus Complex Musings on Arlene Kramer Richards's "The Female Oedipus Complex"

Daniel S. Benveniste, Ph.D.

When Arlene Kramer Richards writes about "The Female Oedipus Complex" (2025), she demonstrates an unusual courage in addressing a theoretical and clinical issue that for many remains controversial, rejected, passe, or completely forgotten. The idea of the Oedipus complex is built upon the stratification of consciousness and unconsciousness, the theory of infantile sexuality, and object relations in the life of the child in the context of the family. Yet each of these foundational ideas have been dismissed or repressed, even in many quarters of modern psychoanalysis. But they've certainly not been dismissed or repressed in Arlene's thinking.

Kramer Richards couches her discussion in psychoanalytic history from Freud's first speculations about the girl's "penis envy as bedrock and suppression of the clitoris as ideal adulthood" to the "present day emphasis on relationships, variability, and individuality" (p. 106). She cites alternative theorists who have proposed alternative paths to adulthood for women based on different identifications and object choices in relation to parents and parenting figures. These alternative paths have proposed different mythic metaphors, such as the myths of Electra and Persephone. The alternative theories are often of great complexity and may well describe the clinical experience of the theorist or the experience of the theorist herself. But in a refreshing paragraph Kramer Richards writes:

"All of this hypothesizes a degree of fantasizing and sophistication of logic characteristic of a psychoanalyst, but, I submit, not of an infant, toddler, or even a three- to six-year-old child. The cognitive capacity demonstrated by this tour de force of reasoning is beyond that of adolescence, even in the most brilliant child. Attributing such mental gyrations to a young child is not supported by any evidence I know of" (pp. 9–10, this volume).

These are the words of someone who obviously knows about children—and not just from reading about them. Kramer Richards speaks in the experience near terms of attachments, the desire to be loved, feelings, identifications, and the importance of being seen and understood. She says:

The Oedipal conflict is determined by the universal experience of attachment to the early nurturer, partly by the infant's genetic endowment, partly by parental characteristics, partly by parental fantasies of the child, personality, and partly by the cultural expectations and restrictions that the child is born into (p. 17, this volume).

We read this and suddenly feel a sense of freedom. Kramer Richards is reminding us that theory is not the same as life, "the map is not the territory." There are multiple maps. And while the maps can be useful, what is important, clinically, is the path taken by the individual, the benefits of that path, and a curiosity about the paths, or roads, not taken. This is where we find old hurts, untapped potential, and new opportunities for a wider, fuller experience of life.

The Oedipus complex first dawned on Freud in his personal analysis when he recalled his childhood love for his mother and his hatred for his father. He then associated it with the basic theme of Sophocles' legend of Oedipus Rex. Around the same time, the 1890s, Freud was struggling with the etiology of hysteria. With his seduction theory he concluded that the "event" of child seduction by an adult resulted in hysteria. Later, with his new theory of infantile sexuality, Freud recognized that the causative factor of psychological disturbance was not the "event" of seduction but rather the "experience" of seduction, and that experience could be caused by an adult seducer or a combination of an adult caretaker and the child's own sexual fantasies. Freud was moving from the physical to the mental, from the brain to the mind, from the event to the experience. He did not deny that children were traumatized by seductions; he was noting that in some situations the trauma resulted from a combination of normal caretaking and the child's normal sexual fantasies. In some situations, normal caretaking might not cross the line into sexual seduction or molestation but still might be sufficiently overstimulating to awaken the child's natural sexual fantasy life to a problematic level.

We have all had patients who were not molested but had parents who were seductive, overstimulating, inappropriate, or blurred generational difference. I am reminded of a girl who became uncomfortably aware of her father's leering eyes when she wore a bikini, of a boy who hated shopping for clothes as his mother always uncomfortably checked the fit of his pants by putting her hand just inside the waistband and pulling on it, of a divorced father who routinely asked his adult daughter to buy sexy lingerie as gifts for his girlfriends, and of a mother who bought her adult son all of his underwear, including sexy underwear, well into adulthood. These examples of Oedipal themes playing out from childhood into adulthood often lead to suffering of various forms in adult sexual development.

Totem and Taboo

From early in his career, Freud noted the remarkable similarity between the images and themes in dreams and fantasies of individuals and the legends and mythologies of ancient cultures. The legend of Oedipus Rex was embraced by psychoanalysis and turned into a point of orientation from which analysts have mined new insights for over a century. In *Totem and Taboo* (1913) Freud imagined the Oedipal scene taking place in prehistoric societies. He said that in prehistoric times a primal despotic father ruled over a small band of people, kept all the females for himself, drove off his adult sons, and battled them when they tried to take his place. Eventually the sons killed the father, delighted in their victory, cannibalized him, and then mourned the loss of their father. Freud said people did this over and over until the repeated event became an archaic memory that is now remembered in our modern minds as the Oedipus complex.

But people do not remember the events that took place in the lives of their ancestors. This one flaw in his theory got in the way of *Totem and Taboo* receiving broader acceptance among psychoanalysts and anthropologists. It is more parsimonious to say we are primates, and we have primate social instincts, including alpha male dynamics that are the basis of the Oedipus complex. Another primate social instinct is copulation interference. Chimpanzee babies stay close to their mothers for years. When the chimpanzee mother copulates, her child will commonly climb onto her back and try to push off the copulating male. This behavior by the chimpanzee youngster is curiously tolerated up until a certain age when a taboo against this interference is enforced by the male with open aggression. We can see some of this dynamic even in humans when young parents are hugging or kissing and their young children come in between to separate them, take one of the parents for himself or herself, or just share in the hug.

Oedipal Themes in Myths Around the World

But why is the great mystery of the soul for all humans

written only in a Greek legend? Did the ancient Greeks hold the secrets of the soul? Do other cultures generate myths and legends of a similar character? Well, yes, they do. But before getting into all that, let's first recognize the basic components of the legend of Oedipus Rex that align with the behavior of children in families. To begin with we see the incest wish and the incest taboo, and the patricidal wish and the patricidal taboo. The wishes, whether conscious or unconscious, are recognized as universal and so are the taboos, even in chimpanzees.

For any of us to even begin to understand psychoanalysis, we must learn to think in metaphor. With regard to the Oedipus complex, the mother is a metaphor for the provision of instinctual gratification; the father is a metaphor for setting limits, educating, imposing rules and laws, and establishing values and institutions; castration is a metaphor for the action of the fathering figure in limit setting; penis envy is a metaphor for wanting the social power of the other. Thus, the Oedipus complex is a metaphor for socialization in which the child learns the social implications of gender difference and generational difference, establishes identifications, and constellates a superego. (Note: The father figure is typically an adult male in the life of the child, while I refer to the "fathering figure" as the person who imposes the prohibitions, sets limits, and educates the child.)

When we think in metaphor, we can see the way a mother can both mother and father her children. We can see the way a father can both father and mother his children. We can see the way gay, lesbian, single or communal parents can both mother and father their children. When the Oedipus complex is no longer Sophocles' truth or Freud's truth or anyone else's truth, it becomes a set of anatomical and developmental markers around which each person finds their own truth and their own suffering in the context of their family.

Returning to the question, why should a Greek legend be the one around which the psyches of all humanity are organized?

The answer, in brief, is it's not. Oedipal themes are found in myths, legends, and folktales all around the world. The themes of dangerous impulses and society's taboos instituted to protect us from them are ubiquitous. There are many myths that are as transparent in their incestuous and murderous family dynamics as the story of Oedipus and many more that only thinly disguise those dynamics.

Sophocles' legend of Oedipus Rex debuted on stage in 529 BCE, but the story components were even more ancient and were part of many folktales that preexisted Oedipus Rex. In Lowell Edmunds's book *Oedipus: The Ancient Legend and Its Later Analogues* (1985), we learn of similar medieval folktales from Turkey, Israel, Iraq, and a Sufi sect in the Sudan. One could easily suggest that the story components of the legend of Oedipus Rex may have been diffused throughout the region, but the further removed geographically, the more compelling are the similarities. Edmunds also found analogous tales among the people of the Ulithi Atoll, now a part of Micronesia; among the Zulus in Africa; among the Malagasy of Madagascar; and among the people of the Antilles in the Caribbean Sea.

When such story components are shared far and wide, we can consider the possibility of diffusion of those components through human contact but must also consider the possibility of a pan-human narrative similar to the ubiquity of hero myths and creation myths, which appear in all human cultures. Even if communities in Micronesia, Africa, or the Antilles heard these stories from visitors, why would they have incorporated them into their own folktales? The answer, as Freud said of Oedipus, is that the story components move us because they find resonance in our own impulses:

> His [Oedipus's] destiny moves us only because it might have been ours—because the oracle laid the same curse upon us before our birth as upon him. It is the fate of all of us, perhaps, to direct our first sexual impulse toward our mother and our first hatred and our first

murderous wish against our father (Freud, 1900, *SE*, IV, p. 262–263).

The story was made up or picked up by cultures far and wide because people around the world recognized themselves within it.

Take, for example, the symbolism of the Chinese dragon. Huaiyu Wang (2015) says the image of the Chinese dragon is more than 5,000 years old. In modern times the dragon is well known to be an auspicious figure that brings good luck, but early Chinese beliefs associated the dragon with the demonic and saw it as an omen of misfortune and disaster. The auspicious and the demonic aspects in the same figure remind us of the psychoanalytic insight that ambivalent attitudes characterize many of our human relations. Wang traces dragon worship into the distant past and identifies the dragon with both the father and the king. He then explains that the ambivalent feelings related to the father and king were managed with rules, laws, prohibitions, and taboos.

Furthermore, Wang explains that Fu Xi and Nu Wa are the mythological ancestors of the Chinese people. They represent yin and yang, as husband and wife but also as brother and sister. Images of Fu Xi and Nu Wa with intertwined serpentine bodies have led Wang to conclude that the serpent bodies of Fu Xi and Nu Wa symbolize two dragons engaged in intercourse. Thus, the dragon contains all the ambivalent feelings of love and hate, affection and resentment, as are also seen in the legend of Oedipus. The dragon is also associated with incest, but unlike the mother-son incest of the Oedipus legend, the pair of Chinese dragons (Fu Xi and Nu Wa) engage in brother-sister incest. In these reflections Wang helps us to see how Chinese dragon worship receives and contains ambivalent feelings of love and hate and symbolizes a conflict between primitive impulses and society's prohibitions. In this way we can see that Chinese dragon worship is also a metaphor for socialization. It represents right order upheld by the

29

king against the repressed primitive impulses that threaten to bring chaos.

Another correlate to the themes of patricide and the taboo against patricide is found in the Chinese legend of Nezha. The tale's ancient roots are 2,000 years old, but it was written in its classic modern form 400 years ago. It is the story of a mischievous and rebellious boy, Nezha, who is in constant mortal combat with his father, General Li Jing. At its heart is the boy's conflict in relation to his father. He harbors anger and resentment toward his father as well as a moral obligation to respect his father as his father. The father hated Nezha from his birth for being ugly and then, later, for bringing problems to the family and for the endless battles with his father. Meir Shahar (2015) writes, "Subversion of authority is the key to the Nezha myth" (p. 5). He explains that Chinese culture places a high value on filial piety in the private realm and loyalty in the political sphere (p. 5). Filial piety means the child behaves dutifully, respectfully, and gratefully toward the parents, and loyalty means the citizens behave subserviently and deferentially toward the ruler or ruling class. While filial piety and loyalty are cultural values that are consciously embraced, they naturally conceal the anger and resentments of the son toward the father and those of the citizenry toward the rulers and ruling class.

In other cultures, the son's love for the mother and hatred for the father are echoed in myths of the separation of the world parents. In a Polynesian creation myth, for example, Rangi, who was heaven and the father, was lying on top of Papa, who was earth and the mother. They had children, but because Rangi was lying on top of Papa, there was no light, only darkness. So, the children made a plan to tear them apart. Tanemahuta put his head on his mother and then, with his feet, he thrust his father up into the skies, high up into the heavens, letting in the light. "No sooner was heaven rent from earth than the multitude of human beings were discovered whom they had begotten, and who had hitherto lain concealed between the bodies of Rangi and Papa" (Long, 1963, p. 93).

In an Egyptian cosmogony, the interfering son is displaced by an interfering father:

The goddess of heaven, Nut, was still lying upon her spouse, the earth god Seb (or Keb). Then the god of atmosphere (or air), her father Shu, shoved himself between them and lifted her up along with everything which had been created, i.e., every god with his boat (p. 99).

In a Minyong cosmogony from India, it is said that Melo, who was a man and the sky, was married to and lying on top of Sedi, who was a woman and the earth. The Wiyus, the ancestral spirits, held a meeting to consider what they could do to keep from being crushed. One of the Wiyus caught hold of the sky and beat him, so he had to flee far into the heavens (p. 106). In these three tales the separation of the world parents gives rise to physical space and light as an analogue to the psychological space and light that comes about in the Oedipal stage of child development.

For many years Frans de Waal studied the chimpanzee colony at the Royal Burgers' Zoo in Arnhem, Netherlands. He observed:

When adults start a mating session the young come rushing up. They jump on the female's back so as to be able to push her partner away or touch him, or they wiggle between the couple. They throw sand at them or, despite their size, conduct intimidation displays. In one instance, Franje's son, Fons, interfered when Nikkie mounted Franje. In this instance, Fons actually bit Nikkie's testicles. And on another occasion, involving the same triad, Fons simply approached, embraced the two and gave Nikkie a kiss (2007, pp. 156–158).

Some years ago, I conducted a small investigation relating to this type of behavior in humans (Benveniste, 2022). I asked the parents of young children, "What is the reaction of your child when he/she sees you and your spouse hugging and/or kissing?" I collected data on 30 children (22 boys and 8 girls). When parents were hugging or kissing, 18 of the children intervened between the two parents. Of those 18, there were 9 who actually pushed out one of the parents. The following are a few examples of the parents' replies:

MA *Girl, 4 years old*
She gets closer to us, and she hugs both of us and says that the three of us have to give kisses to each other. Sometimes she is jealous with her father. She says, "No, no, only me." She wants to push me out and stay with her father.

JN *Boy, 3 years 6 months*
When we are kissing, he comes in between us or he says, "Give my father to me because he is mine." And he hugs and kisses his father.

AA *Girl, 7 years 2 months*
She comes in the bed with us, and in the morning we wake up hugging. But she has a tendency to go more to the father but also to come in between us.

EC *Boy, 2 years 1 month*
When the mother kisses the father, he [the boy] says to his mother, "It's not good to kiss Daddy." "Don't give kisses to Daddy." And then he pulls me and takes me.

Another example of copulation interference approaches the matter in the form of a denied wish—a wish to not interfere. *The Tibetan Book of the Dead* (Evans-Wentz, 1927/1960) is a sacred Buddhist text that prepares the soul for navigating the afterlife realms in order to stay at one with God and not be reborn into the earthly world in the cycle of suffering. *The Tibetan Book of the Dead* dates back to the 1300s. Walter Y. Evans-Wentz's edited translation was based on seven texts and the English translations of Lama Kazi Dawa-Samdup. In the part of the text called "The Closing of the Door of the

Womb," the soul, in the realms of the afterlife, is instructed on how to avoid the cycle of rebirth:

> O nobly born, at this time thou wilt see visions of males and females in union. When thou seest them, remember to withhold thyself from going between them... If at that time, one entereth into the womb through the feelings of attachment and repulsion, one may be born either as a horse, a foul, a dog, or a human being.
>
> If [about] to be born as a male, the feeling of itself being a male dawneth upon the Knower, and a feeling of intense hatred towards the father and of jealousy and attraction towards the mother is begotten. If [about] to be born as a female the feeling of itself being a female dawneth upon the Knower, and a feeling of intense hatred towards the mother and of intense attraction and fondness towards the father is begotten (pp. 177–179).

If we can conclude anything from all of this, it is that the Oedipus complex is a pattern in human behavior embedded in primate social instincts that Freud, with his keen skills of observation, was able to discover first in himself, then in the legend of Oedipus Rex, then in his patients, and then as an organizing myth that is essential to child development and human cultural evolution.

More than one hundred years later, Arlene Kramer Richards reminds us that the map is not the territory, and the pattern is not the person. She helps us to see the patient not simply as an example of the theory but rather as a person with dynamics that may be reflected in one theory or another or may even be the basis for generating new theories.

References

Benveniste, D. (2022). *Libido, Culture, and Consciousness: Revisiting Freud's* Totem and Taboo. New York: IPBooks.

de Waal, F. (2007). *Chimpanzee politics: Power and Sex among Apes*. Baltimore: Johns Hopkins University Press, 1982.

Edmunds, L. (1985). *Oedipus: The Ancient Legend and its Later Analogues*. Baltimore: Johns Hopkins University Press.

Evans-Wentz, W.Y. (1927/1960). *The Tibetan Book of the Dead*. Oxford: Oxford University Press.

Richards, A.K. (2025). *The Female Oedipus Complex*. Chapter in Textbook: Sino-American fourth continuing training program for senior psychotherapists of psychoanalytic orientation in the spring (the 4th course), Wuhan.

Long, C. (1963). *Alpha: The Myths of Creation*. New York: George Braziller.

Lorenz, K. (1963). *On Aggression*. New York: Harcourt, Brace, and World.

Shahar, M. (2015). *Oedipal God: The Chinese Nezha and his Indian origins*. Honolulu: University of Hawai'i Press.

Wang, Huaiyu (2015). The Chinese totem of dragon and the Greek myth of Oedipus: A comparative psychoanalytic study. *International Communication of Chinese Culture*, 2(3): 259–283.

Matrescence: Illuminating Oedipus's Shadow

Christina Biedermann, PsyD, ABAP

> Language shapes perception and expectation; it orga-
> nizes our thinking. When we think about "Oedipus,"
> we think about "castration" and "penis envy," not about
> pregnancy or vagina; when we talk about the "phal-
> lic-Oedipal" phase in little girls, we distract ourselves
> from—and thereby foreclose on—the girl's crucial
> developmental need to identify with her mother (Kulish
> & Holtzman, 2008, p. 184).

In 2008, Nancy Kulish and Deanna Holtzman described the implications of using the myth of Oedipus as a reference point for female development. Nearly 20 years later, in this issue, Arlene Kramer Richards continues this effort in "The Female Oedipal Complex." While doing so, she illustrates the challenge of evolving beyond foundational theories, those Greenberg (2015) referred to as controlling fictions. In my response, I will show how this problem surfaces in the paper and explore the relatively recent addition of matrescence to the psychoanalytic literature as a potential counter to the shadow cast by the Oedipal myth over psychoanalytic under-standings of female development. Investigating *matrescence,*

35

or the process of becoming a mother (Raphael, 1975), with a focus on the complexities of how mothers come to inhabit their maternal bodies, may be one means of countering the Oedipal reference point, as doing so deepens our understanding of what is available to girls as they go through processes of identification and disidentification with their mothers and, in particular, their mothers' bodies.

Oedipus's Shadow

In "The Female Oedipal Complex," Richards begins by reviewing variants of the Oedipal myth for girls, wrestling with how female anatomy is conceptualized in a phallocentric frame (e.g., as damaged, deficient, disappointing) and whether instead to focus on the aspect of Oedipus that represents negotiation of triadic space. Richards describes the various ways of framing girls' relationships to their mothers, including those that center girls' identification with—as opposed to their competition against—them. She ultimately seems most comfortable with the focus on the creation of triadic space and relies on it to interpret four clinical examples. However, she then pans out and suggests that it is not necessarily useful even to view patients as men or women, but rather to approach them as unique beings in need of affective engagement to solve problems. Richards ultimately suggests we evaluate theoretical concepts according to whether they make sense to the patient, whether they fit their stories, and whether they address their pain. She ends with, "Does it make sense to her?"

It is the paradox between Richard's ultimate destination and her clinical examples that I am most interested in, as I believe it illustrates the difficulty of working toward something new within an established frame. The inverse of a frame still evokes the frame as well as the original social systems it was developed in. I will refer to this as Oedipus's shadow.

In the first clinical illustration, a woman struggles with her daughter's reaction to a "strongly Oedipal situation" and is helped by a transference interpretation based in an Oedipal formulation. In the second, a woman has turned away from being physically attractive to her father so as to maintain her mother's affections. And, in the third, Richards attributes change in a patient to the development of insight about the woman's struggle to develop femininity while simultaneously identifying with her father and disidentifying with her mother who was hoarding. In the final example, Richards begins to outline an alternative to an Oedipally-based formulation but then returns to incorporate it. This patient had initially perceived insistence on Oedipal interpretations as attacks on her experience. Richards suggests that recognizing the patient's reality rather than twisting it to fit an Oedipal frame was helpful in so much as it helped the patient understand her ambivalence toward her father in multiple ways including, however, the original Oedipally-derived formulation regarding the incest taboo.

Although Richards concludes this part of the paper with a statement reminding the reader of the range of components that might contribute to the conflicts presented in the clinical examples (e.g., attachment, genetics, parental characteristics and fantasies of the child, personality, and cultural factors), the most explicit features she attends to are aspects of the Oedipal frame (i.e., competition for and fear of parents' affections). As such, readers must wrestle with the gap between the theoretical material Richards presents to challenge the Oedipal frame, her clinical examples, and her ultimate conclusions. One way to understand it is as a demonstration of the difficulty of thinking outside of a dominant frame despite an explicit and educated commitment to do so.

Variants of Oedipus

The myth of Oedipus clearly served a vital function in psychoanalysis, consolidating a model of psychosexual development that paved the way toward psychoanalytic inquiry into ways children use important people in their lives to think, enter into language, define themselves, and separate from their families of origin. It took male children, their minds, and their bodies seriously and centered questions of children's affections, identifications, and sexualities—as well as the ways adults respond to them.

However, the Oedipal myth inevitably reflects Freud's sociocultural position and time. Its Western European origins are clear in its privileging of separation, murderous envy, and desire, and patriarchal in its equation of the male body and power; further, it is rooted in heterosexuality and the gender binary. Most relevant to this paper, Oedipus is a story of an active father and a passive mother (Sidesinger, 2024) that contributes to the vanishing of the maternal body (Balsam, 2013). It does not account for girls' subjective experiences of their bodies, for mothers' experiences of their bodies, or for maternal subjectivity and its impact on girls' development otherwise.

Early efforts to develop variants of Oedipus to account for female development were met with considerable controversy. Carl Jung (1915) briefly attempted to develop an inverse narrative, the Electra Complex, in which girls competed with their rival mothers to attain the attractions of their fathers and, by proxy, gain their fathers' phallic power; however, Freud (1931) dismissed the effort as inaccurate in applying a model based on the male child to female children. He wrote:

> We are right in rejecting the term "Electra Complex" which seeks to emphasize the analogy between the attitude of the sexes. It is only in the male child that we find the fateful combination of love for the one parent and the simultaneous hatred for the other as a rival.

Instead, Freud (1925, 1933) recast female development in terms of the feminine Oedipus attitude and the negative Oedipus complex and then remained largely silent on the subject. As such after insisting on meaningful sexual difference, Freud continued to reify the Oedipal reference point. Feminist scholars have pointed to the Electra Complex and the discussion of it as an inflection point in the development of psychoanalytic theory, a type of placeholder marking—if nothing else—the lack of understanding of female development. Jill Scott (2005) wrote, "Electra *is* complex, even if she does not *have* a complex" (p. 10).

Others have carried forward the tensions in accounting for female development in an Oedipally-derived frame, focusing—for example—on the importance of girls' pre-Oedipal experiences with their mothers (Chodorow, 1978). In these models, girls—relative to boys—are conceptualized as having closer and extended ties to their mothers before whatever separation occurs in the female equivalent of the Oedipal period. Kulish (2022) articulated the implications of psychoanalysis having situated girls and women in this way. She suggested doing so implies girls and women are more needy than boys and men; have weaker superegos; must renounce active, masculine impulses; and need substitutes for, or means of, accessing phallic power, including having a baby. Other scholars have also expressed concerns about locating the uniqueness of girls' experiences in the pre-Oedipal period when resolving the Oedipal dilemma is otherwise conceptualized a means of entering linguistic frameworks, thereby either locking women into phallic linguistic frameworks or out of language altogether (Irigaray, 1977/1985). Stone has questioned the Oedipal framework's requirement of separation from, if not killing off of, mothers as a form of matricide (2012).

In contrast, Kulish and Holtzman (2008) elaborated an alternative Greek myth to address female development, the story of Persephone. In the myth, a young maiden is abducted into the Underworld by Hades while picking flowers. Hades takes her as his spouse, presumably they consummate the marriage and she loses her virginity, and—upon their union—she takes the name Persephone. Enraged, Persephone's mother, Demeter, spreads drought and famine as she searches for her daughter. Zeus directs Hades to release Persephone; however, Hades tricks Persephone into eating pomegranate seeds, which violates the mandate against eating in the

Underworld and, thus, binds her to him. The gods ultimately achieve a compromise in which Persephone spends part of the year with her mother and part of the year in the underworld with Hades.

In adopting the myth and exploring its implications, Kulish and Holtzman (1998; Holtzman & Kulish, 2000, 2003) attempted to address girls' simultaneous identification with and separation from their mothers, their movement from dyadic to triadic relating, as well as unique female concerns associated with the loss of virginity (e.g., the breaking of the hymen), fertility, and periodicity. Kulish (2022) later suggested the myth of Persephone could be used to understand female pleasure and power, as well as applied to the negotiation of conflicting loyalties to two same-sexed parents.

However, like Oedipus, applying the myth of Persephone to female development has not been without controversy. Scholars have discussed whether Persephone's eating of the pomegranate was a voluntary move toward separation (Foley, 1994) or a division of femininity in the service of patriarchy (Irigaray, 1980/1991). As a representation of menstruation and initiation into femininity (Lincoln, 1991), they have considered whether the myth normalizes Hades' abduction and presumed rape of Persephone (Camden, 2011), thus not only eclipsing her subjectivity but also suggesting girls must assume sexuality in a violent patriarchal frame, adapt, and ultimately renounce ties to their mothers.

Mothering in Oedipus's Shadow

Psychoanalytic elaborations of the myths of Oedipus and Persephone both nearly eclipse their mothers. In Oedipus, Jocasta is subject to an unintended pregnancy, her husband banishing their son to a violent death, and then unknowingly bearing four children with her lost son before ultimately committing suicide. In the story of Persephone, Demeter's primary role is destruction borne of helpless rage and adaptation to Hades' behavior. Beyond these two myths, psychoanalytic writers have addressed the consequences of mothers being treated as objects rather than subjects in psychoanalytic theorizing. Benjamin (1995), for example, focused on contributions to sexual functioning, and Hoffman (1996) argued specifically about implications for women's exertion of agency in the service of sexual pleasure. Grill (2019), Sidesinger (2023), and Young (2020) have all written about the clinical consequences of overfocusing on patients' experiences as daughters rather than mothers, exploring analysts' failures to be interested in decisions about mothering. Attempting to confront the psychoanalytic erasure of the female body in particular, theorists have written about the clitoris (Kulish, 1991), menstruation (Kolod, 2010; Lupton, 1993), the uterus (Kostaras, 2021), childbirth (Balsam, 2013), and menopause (Hettlage-Varjas & Kurz, 1995), as well as generated metaphors based on lived experiences of female bodies like the cervix and the speculum (Goodman, 2020).

Further, over the last 10–15 years, psychoanalytic writers have expressed interest in the persistence of the erasure. Balsam (2012; 2015b, 2017, 2018) cites its origins in Freud's rejection of Rank, Adler, and Jung for addressing childbirth and female genitalia and traces it through the denunciations of Hilferdig, Horney, and Rank for including the female body in their developmental theories and into more contemporary writing. In this way, she demonstrates the recapitulation of Freud's "phallocentric certainties" (Balsam, 2013, p. 695) and suggests that the erasure is motivated as a means of delegitimizing, if not altogether undermining, the power of the female body to create life, to expand and to contract, and to birth. She deems it psychoanalysis's "war on women" (Balsam, 2015b).

The Persistence of Oedipus's Shadow

One might wonder what might motivate such apparent commitment. On one hand, it could be attributed to the inevitable reference point of an origin story. As he began to take seriously and organize patients' speech, Freud's use of Oedipus as an organizing myth captured what he was observing of his patients and the world around him. However, returning to Balsam's assertion that the erasure of the female body since has been too persistent to ignore, we might continue to wonder what drives it. Here, Balsam (2015b) and Kulish (Kulish, 2021) cite Julia Kristeva's (1980/2010) work on the abject. Applied to this problem, the abject describes the conflation of the mother—and her body—with the horror in the identity disturbance that arises when considering the corporeal realities of birth and the maternal body that births. Others have cited the impact of similarly dreadful fears in discussions of the uterus as a site of, and potential container for, archaic fears (Kostaras, 2021). Kulish (2022) ultimately goes further and states that some stories are "bulwarks against change, for individuals and for groups" (p. 839). They provide narratives that maintain and protect self-cohesion and esteem, and for groups, they foster cohesion and preserve identity so as to keep others out in the service of maintaining power.

A recent example of how the Oedipal myth is maintained is an article in The American Psychoanalyst (TAP) where MILF (Mothers I Would Like to F---) pornography is used as proof of Oedipal dynamics, and critiques of the use of pornography as evidence for Oedipus are preemptively dismissed as denial, discomfort, or disgust (Ratner, 2024). Barring the possibility that the numbers of adult men the author cites as using MILF pornography are developmentally arrested, perhaps there may be motivations outside of the developmental stage described in the Oedipal myth. Further, the author's denunciation of even potentially legitimate critique magnifies the assertion of power perpetuated by the Oedipal story. Each time we apply the Oedipal myth, we carry forward and are subject to the power structures within it.

Matrescence

Reconsidering maternal subjectivity, contemporary authors have begun linking erotic aspects of the maternal and embodied capacities to mother (Celenza, 2022; Gentile,

2016; Kristeva, 2014). They have suggested girls' identifications with their mothers (Balsam, 2015a; Benjamin, 1986), maternal bodies (Balsam, 1996), and other untold aspects of female development may be important ways of understanding girls' psychic development and correcting the negative implications for girls embedded in psychoanalytic models based in the Oedipal frame. Rather than overfocusing on girls' separation from and subsequent rejection of their mothers and their mothers' non-phallic bodies, these writers argue for attention to the particularities of the female body as means of understanding female development and the patriarchal systems perpetuating its erasure.

One example of increased attention to the maternal body is the recent psychoanalytic focus on *matrescence*, a term developed based on the intersection of the maternal body, maternal subjectivity, and sociocultural factors observed in the study of breastfeeding (Raphael, 1975). Beyond generating theory based on the lived experience of female bodies, Sidesinger (2023) suggests that incorporating matrescence into psychoanalysis is a means of confronting the current sociopolitical moment and interrupting cycles of violence.

Athan and Reel (2015) describe pregnancy, birth, and the postpartum period as accelerated change manifest in cycles of disorientation and reorientation, including in a mother's experience of her physical body. Matrescence describes mothers' processes of integrating these changes into their embodied selves, which ultimately forges the bodies they bring to their daughters' development.

With the concept of matrescence, Raphael and Athan not only deconstruct the process of becoming a mother but also they implicitly articulate the ways motherhood is constituted and situated within existing power structures (Jones, 2024; Sidesinger, 2024). They extract the active act of mothering from the more passive, objectifying frame of motherhood (Rich, 1976; Sidesinger, 2024) and, in doing so, address traumatic objectification and loss of agency (Sidesinger, 2024).

Sidesinger (2023) describes investigating matrescence as a means of recognizing interconnectedness versus subjugation and of linking mother and child versus focusing on either mother or child. Further, she suggests we extend this thinking to include a variety of maternal subjectivities, including step-mothers, mothering post-divorce or after the death of a spouse, and mothers in non-conventional family structures. In these ways, understanding matrescence goes beyond just understanding the transitions of an individual mother and her body to include understanding how society shapes what is ultimately available to girls.

Conclusion

As one means of illuminating Oedipus's shadow, I have argued that we might focus on matrescence as the process that shapes the body a mother inhabits during her daughter's development. Without explicit focus on maternal subjectivities and embodiments, we risk perpetuating the passage into erasure associated with becoming a mother in Western patriarchal cultures (Jones, 2024) and forego opportunity to develop our understanding of girls' development. Returning then to the clinical examples in Richards's paper, I wonder what details, formulations, or interventions might emerge if the particularities of female bodies and subjectivities—both the patients' and their mothers'—were elaborated and conceptualized in terms eclipsed by Oedipus's shadow.

In an interview with Michaela Chamberlain, author of *Misogyny in Psychoanalysis*, Adam Phillips (2023) suggested that to acknowledge the misogyny in psychoanalytic theory would force the field to re-absorb the shame it has cast onto mothers. Similarly, Sidesinger (2023) suggests that recognition of maternal subjectivity is less about promoting insight into a mother's narrative about herself than developing the Other's ability "to imagine, understand, and relate to her as a subject" (p. 296). To re-integrate shame is a formidable task, particularly when attempted alone. I am grateful for the invitation to join Dr. Richards in questioning the relationship between the Oedipal myth and female development, and I hope, in response, to continue the work being done to shift women and mothers from object to subject (Orbach & Eichenbaum, 1995), to explore the psychic impact of developing in a female body, and to generate more expansive theories (Nadler, 2023) into psychoanalytic discourse.

Author Note
Christina Biedermann
https://orcid.org/0000-0001-8180-7639
Illinois School of Professional Psychology at
National Louis University

The author has no known conflict of interest to disclose.

Correspondence regarding this article should be addressed to: Christina Biedermann, PsyD, ABAP. Email: cbiedermann@nl.edu

References

Athan, A., & Reel, H.L. (2015). Maternal psychology: Reflections on the 20th anniversary of deconstructing developmental psychology. *Feminism & Psychology, 25*(3), 311–325.

Balsam, R.H. (1996). The pregnant mother and the body image of the daughter. *Journal of the American Psychoanalytic Association, 44 Suppl*, 401–427.

——— (2013). (RE)membering the female body in psycho analysis: Childbirth. *Journal of the American Psychoanalytic Association, 61*(3), 447–470.

——— (2015a). Oedipus Rex: Where are we going, especially with females? *Psychoanalytic Quarterly, 84*(3), 555–588.

——— (2015b). The war on women in psychoanalytic theory building: Past to present. *The Psychoanalytic Study of the Child, 69*(1), 83–107.

——— (2017). Freud, the birthing body, and modern life. *Journal of the American Psychoanalytic Association, 65*(1), 61–90.

——— (2018). "Castration Anxiety" revisited: Especially "Female Castration Anxiety." *Psychoanalytic Inquiry, 38*(1), 11–22.

Balsam, R.M. (2012). *Women's bodies in psychoanalysis.* London: Routledge.

Benjamin, J. (1986). The alienation of desire: Women's masochism and ideal love. In J. L. Alpert (Ed.), *Psychoanalysis and women: Contemporary reappraisals* (pp. 113–138). Hillsdale, NJ: Analytic Press, Inc.

——— (1995). *Like subjects, love objects: Essays on recognition and sexual difference.* New Haven: Yale University Press.

Camden, V.J. (2011). A story of her own: The female Oedipus complex reexamined and renamed [Review of the book *A story of her own: The female Oedipus complex reexamined and renamed* by Nancy Kulish and Deanna Holtzman]. *American Imago, 68*(1), 139–148.

Celenza, A. (2022). Maternal erotic transferences and the work of the abject. *Journal of the American Psychoanalytic Association, 70*(1), 9–38.

Chodorow, N. (1978). *The reproduction of mothering.* Oakland: University of California Press.

Foley, H. (Ed.). (1994). *The Homeric "Hymn to Demeter": Translation, commentary, and interpretive essays.* Princeton: Princeton University Press.

Freud, S. (1925). Some psychical consequences of the anatomical distinction between the sexes. In *The standard edition of the complete psychological works of Sigmund Freud* (Vol. 19, pp. 248–258).

———— (1931). Female Sexuality. In *The standard edition of the complete psychological works of Sigmund Freud* (Vol. 21, pp. 225–243).

———— (1933). On Femininity. In *The standard edition of the complete psychological works of Sigmund Freud* (Vol. 22, pp. 112–135).

Gentile, J. (2016). Between the familiar and the stranger: Attachment security, mutual desire, and reclaimed love. *International Journal of Psychoanalytic Self Psychology*, *11*(3), 193–215.

Goodman, N. (2020). Increasing psychic space to see something new, to think something new, to be part of a new thought collective: Discovering the female cervix. *International Journal of Controversial Discussions*, *3*, 69–81.

Greenberg, J. (2015). Therapeutic Action and the Analyst's Responsibility. *Journal of the American Psychoanalytic Association*, *63*(1), 15–32.

Grill, H. (2019). What women want: A discussion of "Childless." *Psychoanalytic Dialogues*, *29*(1), 59–68.

Hettlage-Varjas, A., & Kurz, C. (1995). Difficulties in becoming a woman and staying a woman. On the problems of female identity in menopause. *Psyche*, *49*(9–10), 903–937.

Hoffman, L. (1996). Freud and feminine subjectivity. *Journal of the American Psychoanalytic Association*, *44 Suppl*, 23–44.

Holtzman, D., & Kulish, N. (2000). The femininization of the female Oedipal complex, part I: A reconsideration of the significance of separation issues. *Journal of the American Psychoanalytic Association*, *48*(4), 1413–1437.

———— & Kulish, N. (2003). The femininization of the female Oedipal Complex, part II: Aggression reconsidered. *Journal of the American Psychoanalytic Association*, *51*(4), 1127–1151.

Irigaray, L. (1985). *This sex which is not one* (C. Porter & C. Burke, Trans.). Ithaca: Cornell University Press. (Original work published 1977).

———— (1991). *Marine lover of Friedrich Nietzsche* (G. Gill, Trans.). New York: Columbia University Press (Original work published 1980).

Jones, L. (2024). *Matrescence: On the mind/body/spirit transformations of pregnancy, childbirth, and. motherhood.* Bayside: Pantheon.

Jung, C. (1915). *The theory of psychoanalysis.* Chicago: The Journal of Nervous and Mental Disease Publishing Company.

Kolod, S. (2010). The menstrual cycle as a subject of psycho-analytic inquiry. *The Journal of the American Academy of Psychoanalysis and Dynamic Psychiatry, 38*(1), 77–98.

Kostaras, P. (2021). The maternal uterus as the primary object and its role in anxiety. *British Journal of Psychotherapy, 37*(4), 637–654.

Kristeva, J. (2010). *Powers of horror: An essay on abjection* (L. S. Roudiez, Trans.). New York: Columbia University Press,1980.

Kristeva, J. (2014). Reliance, or maternal eroticism. *Journal of the American Psychoanalytic Association, 62*(1), 69–85.

Kulish, N. (2021). The abject: Clinical manifestations of hatred of the feminine. *Canadian Journal of Psychoanalysis, 29*(1), 50–67.

———— (2022). The power of stories. *Journal of the American Psychoanalytic Association, 70*(5), 829–844.

———— & Holtzman, D. (1998). Persephone, the loss of virginity and the female Oedipal complex. *The International Journal of Psycho-Analysis, 79,* 57–71.

——— & ——— (2008). *A story of her own: The female Oedipus complex reexamined and renamed*. Lanham: Jason Aronson.

Kulish, N.M. (1991). The mental representation of the clitoris: The fear of female sexuality. *Psychoanalytic Inquiry, 11*(4), 511–536.

Lincoln, B. (1991). *Emerging from the chrysalis: Rituals of women's initiation*. Oxford: Oxford University Press.

Lupton, M.J. (1993). *Menstruation and psychoanalysis*. Champaign, IL: University of Illinois Press.

Nadler, C. (2023). *Dyking Oedipal logics of sexual difference*. Milan: Zenodo.

Orbach, S., & Eichenbaum, L. (1995). From objects to subjects. *British Journal of Psychotherapy, 12*(1), 89–97.

Phillips, A. (2023). Misogyny in psychoanalysis: Michaela Chamberlain in conversation with Adam Phillips [Video recording]. https://www.freud.org.uk/whats-on/on-demand/talks/misogyny-in-psychoanalysis/

Raphael, D. (1975). *Matrescence, becoming a mother, a "new/old" rite de passage*. Berlin: De Gruyter Mouton.

Ratner, A. (2024). Oedipus returns: Everything you ever wanted to know about MILF's but were too uncomfortable to ask. *The American Psychoanalyst, 58*(1), 10–19.

Rich, A. (2021). *Of woman born: Motherhood as experience and institution* (1st ed). New York: W.W. Norton & Company., 1986.

Scott, J. (2005). *Electra after Freud: Myth and culture*. Ithaca: Cornell University Press.

Sidesinger, T. (2023). Reproductive agency and the transgenerational transmission of trauma. *Contemporary Psychoanalysis, 59*(1–2), 64–85.

———— (2024). Introduction to the Special Issue on Maternal Subjectivity: An Essential Link in Relational-Social Psychoanalysis. *Psychoanalytic Perspectives, 21*(3), 281–305.

Stone, A. (2012). Against matricide: Rethinking subjectivity and the maternal body. *Hypatia, 27*(1), 118–138.

Young, R. (2020). Reclaiming the female body: My journey From a one-person to a two-person psychoanalysis. *The Psychoanalytic Review, 107*(3), 243–265.

Revisiting the Female Oedipus Complex: How Trauma and Gendered Attitudes Also Shape Development

Thomas DePrima

Arlene Kramer Richards begins her paper by framing this as a "conversation about the Oedipus Complex," going on to describe it as "complicated, knotty, sometimes even vitriolic." I appreciate this as it conveys that this is a topic worth *discussing*, and that we should not be content that any particular perspective—or myth for that matter—has already worked it all out. She then takes up the enormous task of summarizing and analyzing the various historical threads of how this topic has been discussed over the past hundred years or so. She distills her own thinking on the topic into a thoughtful perspective on how all children wish to be loved by their parents yet must navigate the limitations to how available this love can be. She emphasizes that one of the complicating factors of receiving such love is the vicissitudes of the triadic situations that arise between the child and her various early love objects. Underscoring the non-universal aspects of development, she draws attention to how particular family dynamics that are at play with a given child will set the stage for developmental lines that have a lifelong impact on her ability to enter into and remain in loving relationships with others. Also underscoring the non-universal aspects of development, she cautions us against seeing any particular person as merely "an example of a class," and in doing so collapsing their individuality.

I would like to pick up on this theme of the non-universal aspects of development and focus on two topics in particular: the impact on development from trauma and from exposure to attitudes regarding gender. Since this issue focuses on the "female Oedipus complex," I will center my discussion on the development of girls. I recognize these issues also impact development in boys and in those who come to have a non-binary gender identity, but I do feel it is useful to have this discussion that specifically centers around girls and their development.

It is also worth acknowledging that our field has a tendency to theorize development through a heteronormative and cisnormative lens, often implicitly though sometimes explicitly. In a similar vein, our theoretical understanding of development allows us to engage with all sorts of family configurations. But there is a tendency to default—explicitly or implicitly—to discussing the Oedipus complex as a drama that unfolds in the mind of a developing child who is raised by a married mother and father. Our developmental model is certainly equipped to consider households with two mommies, or two daddies, or a mommy and a grandma, or a single parent, or divorced parents with all sorts of custody and stepparent arrangements, and households with or without siblings, etc.

I want to clarify that this paper is not intended to examine variations of family configuration and variations in sexual orientation and gender identity in depth. My discussion of these tendencies is mostly motivated by my wanting to draw attention to the unintended consequences when we engage in such oversimplifications. While these tendencies have diminished over time, they still can be seen in the classroom, in supervision, in the consulting room, and in publications. I was once treating a woman who was contemplating pursuing psychoanalytic training. She identified as lesbian and she and her wife were planning on starting a family in the near future. She took a course on child development at an analytic institute and when the Oedipus complex was being discussed, she asked the instructor a question about the implications for development of a child having a set of same sex parents rather than a mother and father. The instructor replied something to the effect of "honestly, I haven't really thought about that". Not surprisingly this was discouraging to my patient on multiple fronts. It made her feel excluded. And perhaps more concerning was how the exchange demonstrated a lack of creativity and flexibility needed to adapt one's models to the diversity found out in the world. My patient did end up pursuing psychodynamic therapy training, but at a different institute.

Having laid out the above considerations, I now come to this paper's main ideas. Trauma is an enormous topic within the realm of psychoanalytic thinking and it has increasingly garnered societal recognition and attention. A 2025 Lancet study that collected data from 204 countries over a span of over three decades found the worldwide prevalence of sexual violence against children (SVAC) to be 18.9% for females. Also significant was the finding of SVAC for males to be 14.8%. Considering the direct impact of trauma as well as the inter-generational impacts, any theorizing about development must be mindful of this reality. So much has already been written about Freud's pivot from the seduction model to his theorizing about infantile psychosexual development including his developing the concept of the Oedipus Complex. I am not interested in focusing now on an apology or a critique of Freud; rather I wish to emphasize how trauma and psychosexual development are not *separate* topics. Along a similar vein, I would like to challenge the tendency to primarily think of trauma as a kind of *interrupter* of development rather than as one of the potential *contributors* to development. In 2023 Avgi Saketopoulou and Ann Pellegrini published a book,

Gender Without Identity, dedicated to examining how gender identity is *acquired*, in particular queer gender identity. Steeped in Laplanche's metapsychology, a significant part of their thesis involves examining the role trauma often plays in such an acquisition. This way of thinking of trauma opens the door for treatments that are still rooted in the psychoanalytic tradition of *exploration*, rather than more restrictively approaching trauma as something which requires repair. I will now present a case of my own that I hope demonstrates this way of thinking about trauma and development.

Ms. S began seeing me initially for once weekly psychotherapy when she was in her early 20s. Soon thereafter we transitioned the frame into twice weekly Transference Focused Psychotherapy (TFP). The main concerns that motivated her to seek treatment were her struggle to enter and sustain fulfilling romantic relationships, her desire to maintain a recently established sobriety from alcohol abuse that began in her early teens, and her hope to quell what had become persistent thoughts of suicide. Ms. S had an extensive history of abuse dating back to childhood. Her parents divorced when she was about 4 years old and her father left the country soon thereafter, leaving her to be raised by her mother. Ms. S suffered emotional neglect and physical abuse at the hands of her mother and her mother's various boyfriends. There were times when these boyfriends would fondle Ms. S and expose themselves to her. There were several instances of her rebuffing their sexual advances only to then be physically attacked by them. Generally, Ms. S found that telling her mother about these abuses only led to halfhearted advice that "men are pigs and all they want is sex, so you better learn to protect yourself" without really elaborating on how a child was supposed to do this and without acknowledging that the role of protecting the child should fall on the parent. It is worth noting though that for all the ways that her parental objects were *not* good enough, there were loving and tender elements to Ms. S's relationship to her mother. It was harder for her to recall positive early life experiences with male caretakers, aside from some very superficial checking-in from her mostly absentee father.

Among other things, these traumatic aspects of her childhood contributed to a kind of precocious wildness in Ms. S. Around the age of 13 she began seeking out older teens to party with, engaging in binge drinking, recreational drug use, and sexual experimentation. This led to a number of experiences in her early teens of having sex with men typically 5–10 years her senior, often while intoxicated. She soon began to realize that anytime she engaged in sexual activity it would bring on a panic attack. This only further reinforced her tendency to have sex while drunk, as this tended to blunt the panic.

Around the time I began seeing Ms. S she had recently begun to identify as a lesbian. Interestingly, throughout the five or so years of our working together, she continued to have sexual attraction towards men and continued to have sex with men. What became apparent was that she had developed a kind of split: she had more flexibility in terms of how she experienced relationships with women, but with men there was always an overriding sexual character to relationships, both intrapsychically and in terms of how things unfolded interpersonally. Also, with men she experienced more visceral sexual attraction compared to woman, and the sex had the quality of being exciting albeit panic inducing. Sex with women tended to feel intimate albeit lacking passion and excitement. In large part her identifying as lesbian spoke to a way in which she could see women as potential life partners, whereas there was no capacity for partnership with men aside from the realm of sexual encounters. In fact she did have several long term relationships with women, at times living together. Whereas encounters with men tended to be fleeting or interrupted. As the treatment continued, she came to see the label *lesbian* as inadequate and eventually came to identify her sexuality as *queer* as this was less restrictive and reductionistic and as it seemed to account more for her complicated stance towards men and women.

As we continued to work together, another layer emerged: unsurprisingly, Ms. S had internalized a view of men from an early age as dangerous and predatory. In response she had cultivated ways to escape being limited to the role of sexual prey, namely she came to see herself as having a potent sexual power over men. Part of this seemed to be a way to achieve a sort of safety in place of danger. Part of it also had a sadistic quality by identifying with the aggressor. There were dreams and sexual fantasies that emerged in which she would engage in a sort sadomasochistic sexual torture of men.

Better understanding her object relationship with men helped explain a dynamic that played out early in the trans-ference. Almost every early session would at some point include her describing past and present-day sexual expe-riences in graphic even pornographic detail. As I drew her attention to this to explore what was going on, she was able to reflect that whenever she meets a new man, there is an immediate pull to "get the sex out of the way." Typically this would literally entail having sex. Once she had had sex with the man, it felt to her like where there once was danger—that the man would overpower her and take sex from her—now there was control: that she had succeeded in seducing them and by virtue of their desire for her she was "in the driver's seat." With me, she seemed to have arrived at an under-standing that I would not literally have sex with her, but by describing her sexual experiences in such detail, it became a kind of proxy by which she could sexually seduced me. While we did explore this component of the transference in depth, there was a persistent uneasiness she felt throughout the time we worked together with regard to who was in control in the room. Sometimes she felt she had succeeded in seduc-ing me, and relished in the ways this made her feel powerful. Other times she felt more insecure about the possibility that I was disinterested or even disgusted by her, leading to wor-ries that I would abruptly cut the treatment short and "throw her out." This seemed to reveal a more subtle layer still, that this pursuit of control through sex appeal was also a defense against being left, much the way her father left her at such a critical age.

Unfortunately, my treatment with her had a somewhat abrupt termination when she moved out of state to pursue a job opportunity. Over the course of her treatment, though, there was a sense that exploring these developmental lines contributed to a greater flexibility she had in how she related to herself and to others, especially with men. She did maintain her sobriety and she did find some enhanced capacity to cultivate friendships and romantic partnerships. Her suicidal urges had also greatly reduced in intensity and frequency. I have hoped to illustrate that Ms. S's trauma history can be seen in multiple ways that are not mutually exclusive. Her tendency to have panic attacks, to split, to dissociate both psychologically and with the assistance of alcohol, and her suicidality speaks to the ways in which her traumas inflicted psychological damage on her psyche. But her trauma also played a central role in her overall development, including her oedipal development. It shaped the emergence of her sexual fantasies—both conscious and unconscious— it contributed to her evolving sense of her identity with respect to her sexual orientation, and it impacted the ways she sought out love and companionship.

The next topic I want to touch on is the impact on development from exposure to attitudes regarding gender. These kinds of attitudes often contain some combination of prescriptive expectations around gender norms as well as beliefs about intrinsic endowment differences between men and women. I, like many before me, would argue that Freud's theorizing (1925) that girls end up with a diminished superego vs boys on account of their differential oedipal task is itself an example of how societal attitudes influenced Freud's observations. Attitudes regarding gender are highly regional, with cultural, ethnic, religious, institutional layers all at play. These attitudes can also vary greatly from household to household and at times vary greatly between parents and caretakers within a single household. Like trauma, this too is an enormous topic.

A 2022 book titled *Psychoanalytic Explorations of What Women Want Today,* edited by Cereijido, Ellman, Goodman, explores the very vast territory of how conceptions of femininity, gender identity, gender dynamics, gender roles, misogynistic power structures all shape how woman develop and move through the world. Arlene Kramer Richards herself penned one of the chapters titled "What women want and what men want of women". I will now present another case that takes a look at just one slice of this topic: how an adult patient came to discover and contend with a set of views about being a woman that she had not even realized she had been internalizing since childhood.

Ms. O began seeing me in analysis around the time she was finishing law school, just as she was set to begin a position with a big law firm. Much of the early work centered around her frustrations around experiencing unfair treatment at work. Another early theme was Ms. O's tendency to treat romantic relationships with a kind of adversarial stance. Ms. O is bisexual and whether she was in a relationship with a man or a woman, she tended to feel like there was always a power imbalance inherent in relationships, and she was determined to be the person occupying the position of higher power.

As we explored these tensions a number of childhood associations emerged. Ms. O spoke about the unfair treatment from her parents she experienced compared to her younger brother. She was expected to set the table and wash the dishes while her brother was allowed to watch tv and play games. He was allowed to date as an early teenager whereas she was discouraged from dating until she went off to college etc. Ms. O remembers a few times she tried to address the unfairness, but the prevailing response was some iteration of "there are ways girls and boys are different, so you can't expect us to treat you and your brother exactly the same". This created a lot of resentment, much of it conscious. But it also seemed to contribute to a less conscious sensibility in which Ms. O was primed to see future relationships as being inherently unfair and power-imbalanced. And I believe this exacerbated her struggle with the unfairness present in her job environment, and it contributed to the characteristic unbalance of power present in her earlier romantic relationships.

Eventually Ms. O entered into a relationship with a woman that was surprisingly different in character. Her partner tended to be deferential, which Ms. O initially experienced as a kind of weakness. But eventually what emerged was a relationship that felt more mutual, more cooperative, more collaborative, than Ms. O had ever experienced before. Somewhat to her surprise the relationship matured and eventually they married. Within a few years, Ms. O had become pregnant via IVF, and a huge part of our work together then involved working through thoughts and feelings brought up throughout her pregnancy.

Generally speaking, Ms. O had viewed herself as a fairly *liberal* woman, in the tradition of third wave feminism: rejecting prescriptive norms and celebrating individual freedom and empowerment. She felt she arrived at this set of principles mostly through exposure during her educational, professional, and social journeys.

This was in contrast to her experience of her parents as being *old fashioned and conservative.* Much to Ms. O's surprise, as she traversed the path of becoming pregnant and anticipating the birth of her child, she found herself repeatedly grappling with questions having to do with gender roles and gender norms. More than just grappling, she found herself feeling a kind of pull to identify and align with certain gendered norms that she did not recognize as belonging to herself. This was bringing about increasing intrapsychic tension and at times tension with her wife. One example was when Ms. O and her wife were deliberating about whether to move to a new neighborhood. Her wife preferred staying put while Ms. O wanted to move to a more expensive neighborhood to gain access to a better school district. Eventually, Ms. O in a fit of frustration declared "as our boy's mother, it's my job to make sure he attends a good school!" Both Ms. O and her wife were taken aback. Stating the obvious, Ms. O *and* her wife were both going to be the baby's mother, albeit with the asymmetry introduced by Ms. O being the one carrying the pregnancy. But also contained in the statement was the idea that ensuring the child has a good school is a *mother's* responsibility, as opposed to the *other parent/father*. This became a recurring theme in which Ms. O could not help but to conceptualize the family unit with herself as the *mother*, her partner as the *father*, and with a set of expectations about whose job is what.

In exploring this material new associations came forth. Ms. O's own mother was very much the one in charge of ensuring the well-being of the children and in effect ran the household. Even though Ms. O's parents both worked full time, it was her mother who would get her ready for school, take her to the doctor, pick out the school she would attend. As the pregnancy advanced, Ms. O began to worry about how to handle work and family responsibilities. She stressed over the idea of taking more than a few weeks of maternity leave but she also felt tremendous guilt imagining a scenario of "abandoning" her newborn for someone else to look after. When discussing this topic with her mother, she discovered her mother herself only took a few weeks of leave before returning full time to work. Interestingly this was a more nuanced position than could be captured by just seeing her mother as *old fashioned* or *conservative*. Ms. O came to see that on the one hand her mother did very much identify with the gender norm that expects a mother to be the primary, nurturing caretaker of the baby. But, as the first women in her family in several generations to have a full time job herself, Ms. O's mother also identified with the idea that women need to fight for their spot in the workplace. This combination sets up the kind of impossible stance women often find themselves in wherein they must *do it all* and somehow *do it all without compromise,* including fully occupying the roles of *working mom* and *caretaker mom.* Not surprisingly, Ms. O was feeling trapped by this configuration and she struggled to see a tenable way forward.

There was another interesting way that this topic made its way into the treatment. I, myself, became a first time father about a year prior to Ms. O becoming pregnant. When I took my own paternity leave, she became enraged and nearly fired me. At the time, I mainly understood this as her struggling with feelings of abandonment and perhaps feelings of competition as my attention would be diverted to my own child. In light of the above material though, I did come to also see part of Ms. O's reaction as containing the gendered sentiment that taking care of the baby does not fall to the father. So why should I need to take paternity leave? And going one step further, some envy that I, as a father, might provide more hands-on parenting than she had received from her own father. She and I did return to thinking about this episode and there were fantasies she had that my wife was doing all the hard work while I was essentially taking something akin to an extended vacation to "have fun" with the baby. In retrospect she was quite taken aback and even ashamed of how activated she became.

One of the more interesting aspects of this material was Ms. O's coming to realize the many ways she had unconsciously identified with her mother, especially since consciously she preferred to see herself as being more in counter-identification when it came to attitudes around gender. She also found that exploring her own impossible dilemma brought about some newfound appreciation for the similar struggle her mother had to navigate in her own life. Exploring this material did help Ms. O introduce some more flexibility and grace into her approach of how to navigate the transition into motherhood and the demands that come along with it. And it gave her much to think about with respect to how she wants to raise her own son.

On a final note, I would like to revisit Arlene Kramer Richards's encouragement to allow ourselves "to see the uniqueness in each patient rather than see the person as an example of a class." Ironically, what we often find when we do this is that there are a set of formative experiences in which our patients were treated by her caretakers and by others in a way that negated her *uniqueness*, and in which she was treated as *an example of a class*. This ends up being an area where the impacts of trauma and gendered attitudes overlap. Both have the potential to exert an impinging, restricting effect on development. I believe this is one way treatment offers therapeutic potential. When we truly listen to and "see the uniqueness in each patient" we can avoid recapitulating old experiences and instead can achieve a novel and mutative developmental experience with our patients. One of the most important ways for an analyst to refine their ability to be attuned to a given patient is to be a voracious consumer of stories. We do this when we listen to our patients, our friends, our family members, our neighbors, and when we consume fiction, nonfiction, stay abreast of current events, etc. Returning to the topic of this issue, we do this when we more broadly listen to women.

References

Cagney, J. et al. (1990–2023) Prevalence of sexual violence against children and age at first exposure: a global analysis by location, age, and sex (1990–2023). *The Lancet,* Volume 405, Issue 10492, 1817–1836.

Cereijido, M., Ellman, P.L., & Goodman, N. (Eds.). (2022). *Psychoanalytic Explorations of What Women Want Today: Femininity, Desire and Agency.* New York,: Routledge.

Freud, S. (1925). Some psychical consequences of the anatomical distinction between the sexes. *SE* 19:241–258.

Saketopoulou, A. & Pellegrini, A. (2023). *Gender without Identity.* New York, NY: The Unconscious in Translation.

Response to "The Female Oedipus Complex" by Arlene Kramer Richards
Little Girls and Little Boys, Women and Men, Who Are We?

Merle Heidi Molofsky

In this meticulously researched and well-documented essay, Arlene Kramer Richards offers an account of the history of psychoanalytic exploration of female sexuality, of what little girls experience in their early sexual awakenings, their early desire, and how those early thoughts and feelings manifest in adulthood, in women. She also offers her own theorizing regarding female psychosexual development, the formation of early sexual desire.

Importantly, she pays attention to psychoanalytic language used in discussing female psychosexual development. Of course, the term most commonly used by psychoanalysts in discussing later stages of emerging childhood sexuality is "Oedipus complex." Another term that Kramer Richards uses is "triadic." Kramer Richards also refers to the term used to describe particularly female psychosexual development, the "Electra complex". I will discuss the implications of this term shortly.

I prefer the term "triadic." Since the classic Oedipus complex, as described by Sigmund Freud, is that of a little boy whose first love is his mother, a little boy who realizes he has to compete with his father to win the exclusive love of his mother, therefore risking the punitive wrath of his father, whom the boy fears might castrate him, is gender-specific, a term that describes a child competing for a parent's love with the other parent that is gender-neutral is "triadic."

The most common type of a nuclear family, a "traditional" nuclear family, is composed of a cis-gender mother, a cis-gender father, and a child, perhaps more than one child. Thus, a child is embedded in a triadic situation of two adults with the child. In her summary of the developmental factors for the child in this situation, Kramer Richards points out that the child may experience a spectrum of desires for both mother and for father, for Mommy and for Daddy. As each parent is desired, each parent also is a rival.

Kramer Richards focuses on the actual context of a child's desire. Since the theme we are discussing is female psychosexual desire, when I refer to a child, I will consider the child to be a girl and use the pronouns indicating the child is a girl. Kramer Richards notes that the child is aware of her own genital, her genital sensations, and wants genital stimulation. She not only wants to provide genital stimulation to herself, but she also wants her early love objects to provide genital stimulation for her.

Kramer Richards elaborates on the ramifications of a little girl wanting genital stimulation from her love objects. Most little girls may want to grow up and marry Daddy. Some little girls may want to grow up and marry Mommy. Some little girls may want to marry both Mommy and Daddy. Complicating this broadening spectrum is the fact that attractive traits found in one parent may also be seen in the parent of the opposite sex. Kramer Richards focuses on one particularly important issue for little girls. Both little girls and little boys find their first love object to be Mommy. Yet while most little boys retain Mommy as their first love object, and want to grow up and marry Mommy, most little girls find themselves giving up Mommy, their first love object, for an increasingly important love object, Daddy.

I think perhaps the most difficult aspect of the switch from wanting to grow up and marry Mommy to wanting to grow up and marry Daddy is the little girl's establishing her own gender identity. To feel female, a little girl has to identify with her same sex parent, Mommy, and thus, she has to identify with her Mommy's choice of sexual partner, she has to want to grow up and marry Daddy, to be just like her Mommy.

A particular insight that Kramer Richards offers is that psychoanalysts think like psychoanalysts, aware of a complex body of theory, and who usually have significant clinical experience with adults who speak of their memories of their childhood, yet, in contrast, an infant/toddler/three- to six-year-old child may think, feel, and experience in a significantly different way. Of course, some psychoanalysts work with children, even very young children. They need to be able to empathize with, perhaps even identify with, the very young child.

I serve on the Advisory Board and faculty of the Harlem Family Institute (HFI), which is located in New York City. HFI describes itself as offering community services "for children, their parents and adults in need, providing affordable long-term therapy in neighborhood schools and community centers." In its mission statement, HFI says, "The Institute takes psychoanalytic work out into the community where it gives youngsters a safe space to voice their feelings, learn to use their strengths to manage the challenges they face each day, and discuss new ways to relate to the world."

As a faculty member, over many years I have supervised a number of HFI candidates who have worked with young children. A few of the candidates actually worked with children in the three-to-six-year-old range, children attending kindergarten and first grade public schools, although most of the children they worked with were older. Psychoanalysts and psychoanalytic candidates who work clinically with young children may use a number of techniques such as sand tray play, art therapy, the squiggle game, collaborative story-telling, playing competitive games, playing with toys, and in so doing, hear children share their phantasies, tell anecdotes about family life, and of course share their deepest feelings. Yes, working psychoanalytically with young children means that the clinician draws on a bank of psychoanalytic theory, and clinical experience with adults. Nonetheless, these clinicians also have direct interactions with young children and learn from the children themselves how to work meaning-fully with them.

Playing and Reality, (Tavistock 1971) by D.W. Winnicott is a masterpiece most psychoanalysts can draw on if they want to consider how to work with children, and Melanie Klein and Anna Freud specifically wrote about working psychoanalyti-cally with children.

There are quite a number of more recent books written by psychoanalysts that address how to work psychoanalytically with children, such as *The Psychoanalyst and the Child: From the Consultation to Psychoanalytic Treatment*, by Michael Ody, Routledge, 2019; *The Thinking Heart: Three Levels of Psychoanalytic Therapy With Disturbed Children*, by Anna Alvarez, Routledge, 2012; *Working With Parents Makes Therapy Work*, by Kerry Kelly Novick and Jack Novick, Rowman & Littlefield, 2005.

Michael Eigen has written most eloquently about exploring feelings in psychoanalysis in *Feeling Matters,* Routledge, 2007. His book is quite useful in considering the necessity of addressing feelings in psychoanalytic work and readily applies to working with children as well as with adults. Facilitating young children becoming able to identify and explore their innermost feelings is a lifelong gift those children will be able to use.

In her summary of the three clinical cases she wrote about, Kramer Richards paid exquisite attention to the feelings of her analysands. In doing so, she exemplifies what Michael Eigen observes and recommends. As I ruminated over the empathy Kramer Richards has for her analysands, and Eigen's focus on how much feeling matters, I remembered a famous line from the 1949 play, *Death of a Salesman*, by Arthur Miller: "Attention must be paid!" Considering the triadic struggles that are both intrapsychic and externally occurring in reality, we must pay attention! There is no escaping childhood feelings of sexual desire, love, rivalry, inadequacy, fear of loss of a loved parent, fear of abandonment, fear of punishment by a rival, fear of mutilation, shame, guilt, anxiety, and a smorgasbord of defenses to ward off feeling.

I was impressed with Kramer Richards's approach to the little girl's experience by turning to mythology, just as Sigmund Freud did when he considered triadic struggles and used the term Oedipus complex. It is important that Sigmund Freud was a man, and his thoughts about childhood focused on boys. Arlene Kramer Richards is a woman, and is the Editor, with Lucille Spira, also a woman, of *Myths of Mighty Women*, Karnac, 2015. She knows mythology and is profoundly aware of images of women in mythology. Thus, as she discusses the childhood triadic experience faced by little girls, she considers not only the well-established psychoanalytic concept, the Electra complex, she also contrasts Electra with Persephone.

In 1915, Carl Jung introduced the concept of the Electra complex in girls, paralleling the Oedipus complex in boys. The Greek myth involving Electra is worth understanding. Electra and her brother Orestes were the children of Clytemnestra and Agamemnon. Electra and Orestes believed that their mother Clytemnestra conspired with her lover, Aegisthus, to murder her husband, Agamemnon, and seize his throne, which indeed happened. So, the sister and brother murdered their mother, Clytemnestra, to avenge their father. Thus, the term "Electra complex" describes the feelings and phantasies of a little girl who wants to murder her mother because she loves her father.

Kramer Richards offers us the myth of Persephone, daughter of Demeter and Zeus, as a more fitting image, a more powerful "mighty woman" than Electra. Persephone was a fertility earth goddess, worshipped in Greece in the Eleusinian mystery cult. She descended into the underworld every year, joining her husband Hades, causing winter, and returned every spring, bringing vegetation, thus feeding the world, to rejoin her mother, Demeter, who was the goddess of agriculture and harvest. Thus, Persephone is very much like her mother. Kramer Richards refers to a paper by Kulish and Holtzman, describing the myth as focused as a girl's separation from, and loss of, her mother. Thus, the girl is vulnerable to feeling abandoned by her mother. A girl who grows to adulthood, and marries, uses her husband as a substitute for her mother. The little girl wants closeness with both her mother and her father.

Kramer Richards explores a little girl's ambivalence regarding staying close to her mother, aligned with her mother. She says that "a girl repeats her ambivalent attachment to her mother in her relationships with female friends." She cites Butler's idea of femininity as being based on a girl's incomplete mourning for loss of her mother as a sexual love object.

I found myself uneasy as I considered these ideas about a little girl's ambivalence and loss regarding her love for her mother. It seemed to me we might wind up pathologizing being female, being feminine, as girls grow up and become women.

Kramer Richards provides a useful summary of the importance of early childhood in shaping a woman's adult life, since psychoanalytic theorists from various backgrounds agree that this is so. They may emphasize different phases, but acknowledge, correctly, that early childhood shapes adult identity. Kramer Richards identifies key elements, such as attachment, separation anxiety, triangulation regarding love and hate of parental figures, centrality of self-esteem, and trauma. She acknowledges that some theorists try to integrate various phases and experiences into an overall theory of development.

I offer another myth, that of Cassandra, that we might consider. Here is a poem I wrote many years ago about Cassandra:

The Ecstasy of Cassandra

She who refused the marriage bed of a god
For a certain inviolability
Cannot restrain her tongue
From echoing her mind.
The gods have no fear of virgins.
She squats as if in childbirth
At the edge of the sea
Contemplating her rape by a king,
Her exile, her death
By sword.
A stranger, seeing her swoon-misted eyes,
Her crescent smile,
Believed her a new-made bride.

Published in
Mad Crazy Love: Love Poems and Mad Songs,
by Merle Molofsky, Poets Union Press, 2011,
ISBN 970-0-557-75404-5

In considering the myth of Cassandra, I wonder if sexuality is the most important element in adult female experience or is autonomy even more important. Do we project our expectations of the centrality of sexuality onto women, as if femininity, being female, is more important than any other aspect of an adult woman's life?

Or perhaps sexuality indeed may be central to all adult life, women and men both.

Or perhaps our cultural expectations are such that men have autonomy and complexity, but women primarily are child-bearers and nurturers.

Yet Kramer Richards is keenly aware of cultural influences. She points out that the Oedipal conflict is Freud's main story line, that he wrote about "hysterical" women and used his own self-analysis. Kramer Richards identifies the need for self-esteem, recognizes intersubjectivity as part of the clinical dyad experience, and values the need for unity. She acknowledges the need for infant observation.

I taught a human development class at a psychoanalytic institute for many years, focused on early infancy through the triadic conflict, and collected "cute true stories" that I shared with the students. I now will share three stories with the IJCD readers.

A four-year-old boy said to his mother, "Mommy, when I grow up, I will have breasts just like you." His mother spent a moment contemplating what to say, and, wisely answered, "Only girls grow up to be women and have breasts. You are a boy. You will grow up to be a man like your father, and you will have hair on your chest like Daddy has." Her son was delighted with her answer.

Another four-year old boy said to his mother, "Mommy, you are the most beautiful woman in the world. I love you. When I grow up, I will marry you." His mother spent a moment contemplating what to say, and wisely answered, "I am already married, I am married to Daddy. When you grow up and are a man, you will meet many beautiful women. You will meet a woman you fall in love with, and you will marry her, and you will be very happy." The little boy was very happy with her answer.

A little girl reported to her mother her discomfort on seeing a little boy's penis for the first time. The little girl showed no feelings of penis envy. On the contrary, she expressed pity for the little boy, that he had some sort of excrudescence on his genital. She expressed pride in her own smooth genital.

In Kramer Richards's summary of her clinical cases, she says, "I hope that these examples lead clearly to the suggestion that individual experiences of what has been called the Oedipus conflict is determined partly by the universal experience of attachment to the early nurturer, partly by the infant's genetic endowment, partly by parental characteristics, partly by parental fantasies of the child, personality, and partly by the cultural expectations and restrictions that the child is born into."

And thus, we have the inescapable nature nurture question, and the cultural environment. The more we are immersed in theory, in knowledge, the more we question. There is no "Guide for the Perplexed" for us. There only is our capacity to wonder, to think, to feel, to accept, to rebel, to remember.

Remember... . What do we remember? Our studies, our readings, our teachers, our clinical experience, our sense of our own expertise? And, importantly, our childhood? Is knowledge personal?

Kramer Richards shows a true sensitivity to diversity and uniqueness of individual experience. She truly listens to her analysands and respects their individuality and depth. She recognizes we learn from our analysands when we listen.

I gleaned wonderful gems of insight from her, as she points out that feelings are different from what else we learn.

"Psychoanalysis becomes one and myriad."

Since paying attention to feelings is essential, "that attention, both cognitive and emotional, is the power of psychoanalysis."

"...[T]heoretical concepts fit the particular patient at the particular moment."

Our encounter with each analysand can modify our view of the world as we empathize, so that "how what we hear modifies our own feelings as well as our cognitive understanding."

"The way we understand women changes as the culture that shapes us changes so that over space and over time, different theories seem to fit our patient's needs."

This last particular gem reminded me of a memory of something that happened when I was a psychoanalytic candidate in the 1970's. We were discussing the Dora case, and I was appalled. How could we accept Freud's view that Dora was aroused by Herr K's embracing her, that she enjoyed feeling his erection, that she wanted to kiss him? Herr K. had been smoking a cigar. Perhaps she found his cigar breath offensive. But Freud himself smoked cigars, and he may have thought that cigar smoking was manly and enticing to young women. How could Freud have overlooked Dora's admiration of, and desire for, Herr K's wife's "adorable white body"?

I voiced my thoughts in class, and the instructor and my classmates dismissed my ideas. One classmate recommended that I read *Psychoanalysis and Feminism* (Pantheon Books, 1974) by Juliet Mitchell, to understand that my feminist approach was interfering with my appreciation of Freud, and another classmate began referring to me as "the feminist."

What psychoanalytic theories would have helped us further understand Dora during my time as a candidate in that institute class? What psychoanalytic theories would help us understand Dora today? What psychoanalytic theories would help us understand the dynamics in that institute class today?

Kramer Richards's scholarship and knowledge is impressive. I learned a great deal reading her article. I (not so humbly) would like to recommend one more addition to her wonderful array of references, *Female Identity Conflict in Clinical Practice*, an anthology of articles by Doris Bernstein, edited by Norbert Freedman & Betsy Distler, Jason Aronson Press, 2005, Northvale, New Jersey.

Desire, Identity and The Female Oedipus Today: On Arlene Kramer Richards's 'The Female Oedipus Complex'

Adriana Prengler

Since the beginnings of psychoanalysis, the Oedipus complex has been seen as a central, structuring point in the development of identity, sexual differentiation, the construction of desire, the establishment of the symbolic law, and insertion into socialization. However, few dimensions of Freudian thought have been so vigorously debated, elaborated, and questioned as the female Oedipus. The question of femininity, the girl's relationship with mother and father, the passage between primary and secondary bonds, and the symbolic function of maternity have been revisited throughout the history of psychoanalysis from clinical, cultural, and gender perspectives.

The debate surrounding the female Oedipus complex continues to be one of the most controversial nuclei of psychoanalytic thought. More than a century after Freud's formulations, Arlene Kramer Richards's text, *The Female Oedipus Complex*, brings back to the contemporary scene the need to reconsider this problem not only in its theoretical dimension, but also in its clinical and cultural dimensions, as well. Kramer Richards proposes an approach that restores the structural complexity of the female Oedipus in a context where identities and desires present themselves in forms broader than those upon which classical theory was built.

In this context, her article constitutes a highly valuable and timely contribution. It recovers the discussion of the female Oedipus not merely as a historical vestige of early Freudianism, but as an essential clinical organizer whose meaning is continually reactivated in the transference and in the singular ways each woman negotiates their place in the original love triangle.

At a time when many people live their gender identity as a structuring center beyond the chosen sexual object, both clinical work and theory require us to reconsider how the Oedipus is constituted today and to analyze whether we can still speak of the Oedipus as a universal matrix or, rather, as a plural field of possible configurations.

Kramer Richards expands the female Oedipal complexity through different lenses, mentioning key authors who have developed the topic. She illustrates this with clinical vignettes from her own professional experience inviting readers to deepen their understanding of the female Oedipus complex.

According to the dictionary of the Real Academia Española, the etymological root of the word *complejo* (complex) comes from the Latin *complexus*, meaning "to embrace" or "to intertwine." It implies a composition of heterogeneous, multiple, interwoven elements. Thus, Kramer Richards states that we cannot conceive of a single theory of the Oedipus complex, a point sustained by the term's etymology itself. The Oedipus complex is constituted as a fact made up of interlaced aspects and, from the Freudian conception, when we refer to the female Oedipus complex, the displacement of libido from the primordial maternal love object to the paternal object makes it even more complex.

In her article, Kramer Richards brings the Oedipus theory back into focus as a structuring axis of psychic development, something that seems to have been relegated to a less relevant plane in some psychoanalytic training programs, and which I believe, remains a structuring concept of the psyche, alongside narcissism and identification.

Kramer Richards enters into dialogue with Freud and with an entire tradition of psychoanalysts that includes Horney, Kulish and Holtzman, Buchberg, Blass, Maguire, among others. Her central thesis holds that the female Oedipus cannot be reduced to a single explanatory model, nor to anatomical binarism, nor to a linear narrative about penis envy or castration. She also argues that the girl does not necessarily abandon her love for the mother when she chooses the father as a new love object; rather, she is confronted with a tension between both bonds. She describes how the shift from love for the mother to love for the father is not a simple substitution but an interweaving of bonds, identifications, and mourning. In that movement, the girl does not abandon maternal love; she transforms it: she both loves and enters a rivalry with the mother, desires the father, and fears losing the love of both. Her text is inscribed in a line that runs from Freud to object relations theories, emphasizing clinical singularity and cultural variability. That coexistence of desires and rivalries constitutes the female Oedipal plot.

Her clinical vignettes reveal how the Oedipus is reactivated transgenerationally and how each woman negotiates her place between two figures of love and identification, showing that the triangular conflict does not obey a universal or rigid order but is inscribed in subjective and cultural singularities.

From this perspective, it is pertinent to mention the dimension of psychic transmission between generations. As René Kaës argues, we inherit not only traits or mandates but also unconscious alliances and pacts that distribute psychic functions within the family group, sustaining zones of the unthought and of desire that may reappear as Oedipal repetitions (Kaës 2012). In turn, the contribution of Nicolas Abraham and Maria Torok on the crypt and the phantom allows us to conceive that certain unresolved losses and family secrets can return as intrusive presences in the psychic life of descendants, shaping particular ways of loving, engaging in rivalry, excluding, or feeling excluded (Abraham & Torok). From this vantage point, Oedipal reactivation is not reducible to an intrapsychic dynamic but can be read as an enactment of an inherited scene in which each subject reinscribes their place in the generational and affective chain. The clinical vignettes presented in Kramer Richards's text—Y., Sara, and Martine—illustrate variations of the female Oedipus and show how each subject uniquely organizes desire, identification, and fantasies in relation to parental love.

Kramer Richards's reading thus offers an opportunity to revisit the Oedipus today, in a world in which the experience of gender and identity has diversified. We must admit that although Freud conceived the Oedipus complex as a universal structure, contemporary thinking compels us to recognize the need to rethink that structure in the light of modern cultural transformations, without losing sight of its symbolic value as a matrix that organizes desire and sexual differentiation.

According to Freud's formulation, the Oedipal scene posits sexual differentiation, the prohibition of incest, and the institution of the law of a third as essential conditions for integration into culture. Female development is subordinated to the male; the girl appears defined in terms of a lack, of an "incomplete" anatomy that would determine her position in relation to desire. In *Three Essays on the Theory of Sexuality* (1905) and "Some Psychical Consequences of the Anatomical Distinction Between the Sexes" (1925), Freud maintains that the girl discovers her lack of a penis and reacts by displacing her libido from maternal to paternal love. In this way, femininity would be structured by penis envy, and its resolution by the acceptance of maternity as symbolic substitute for the absent organ. This interpretation reduces female experience to the negative of the male model, generating a multitude of critiques within psychoanalysis itself.

From my point of view, it is entirely understandable that this proposal of penis envy has provoked so much controversy. Why should we think today that the girl is defined by what she lacks and not by what she is, what she feels herself to be, and her singular ways of loving and desiring? Why assume it is the girl who envies the penis, and not the boy/man who envies pregnancy, childbirth, breastfeeding?

In contemporary culture, the penis has lost part of its value as a univocal symbol of power and subjective plenitude. As authors such as Alizade (2007), Glocer Fiorini (2010), and Butler (1990) have argued, the phallus—more than the anatomical penis—operates as a signifier of desire, recognition, and symbolic agency, so its "possession" is not circumscribed to a male body. Thus, subjective potency progressively detaches from anatomy and is articulated with modes of being, desiring, and inhabiting the body.

It would therefore seem that we can no longer sustain the traditional notion of the desire for a child as a substitute for the penis when maternity has ceased to be a symbolic destiny and has become a choice—something that also obliges us to separate reproductive function from the constitution of female identity and from the "resolution" of the Oedipus.

Kramer Richards revisits the Freudian tradition and its later developments, illustrating them with clinical vignettes: In the case of Y., she observes how infantile desire within the Oedipal conflict is reactivated across generations through the bond between daughter and father. The girl who longs to be "the most loved" is revived in the mother, who confronts her own place as excluded daughter. In the vignette of Sara, a compulsion to accumulate objects seems to represent her ambivalent identification with the mother and a way of defending herself against the fear of losing her femininity.

In Martine, rivalry with the mother and the search for the father's love reveal the persistence of an un-mourned loss that is perpetuated in adult relationships, showing how Oedipal structure is reactivated at each experience of exclusion or loss of love.

Through these cases, Kramer Richards demonstrates that the clinical manifestations of the female Oedipus mean working with simultaneous, contradictory desires, far from obeying one linear sequence. The girl does not choose between mother or father; rather, she tries at all costs to preserve both as objects of love and identification. This tension—formulated by Freud as ambivalence—acquires in Kramer Richards's an amplified dimension: being loved by both parents and loving both is an originary fantasy that no Oedipal resolution fully suppresses.

The reference to the myth of Persephone is interpreted in her proposal not as a forced passage to heterosexuality, but as a metaphor of double belonging: remaining tied to the mother while entering a new order of bonds. The myth thus expresses the wish to preserve the primary union without renouncing it, while moving towards heterosexuality. This ambivalence in the female Oedipus seems to differ from the male model, where the father appears as an intrusive figure in the child's illusorily exclusive relationship with the mother. We can say that the female Oedipus is configured as a dialectic between permanence and loss, between identification and desire, in which—far from resolving a conflict—one must learn to inhabit it. These ideas open the view to a multiplicity of ways in which each woman—and today, we might say, each person—negotiates affective belonging, identity, and desire.

Extending the frame even further, in light of new gender identities, the classical Oedipal theory proves insufficient. The chosen love object no longer seems to be the primary factor. For many people today, identity as the central axis is independent of the choice of object. Although anatomy-based identity has traditionally been the structural foundation of desire, today anatomy has ceased to be the center of identity, which is no longer necessarily conceived within the man/ woman binary.

In "On Narcissism: An Introduction" (1914) Freud had already anticipated that object love is supported by narcissism: the subject loves what they would like to be or once were. Hence identification precedes desire and object choice. I still consider it valid, following Freud, to think that identity—being a man, being a woman, being a person—is constituted in the fabric of early identifications, while object choice represents a second operation derived from that first experience of identity.

Among a growing number of adolescents and young adults, we observe a heightened preoccupation with defining one's identity, an interest in the self, independent of anatomical body type or the gender of a romantic partner. For many, the question of identity—"Who am I?" (Am I a man? A woman? Both? Or something else?) —overshadows their chosen love object, as if the gender of their partner were irrelevant.

Traditionally, when someone spoke about a sexual experience, a relationship, or a romantic encounter, the gender of the partner was taken for granted and functioned as an almost self-evident fact: if the person identified as heterosexual, they spoke of "the other sex"; if they identified as homosexual, they referred to a partner of "the same sex." Today, however, among a growing number of adolescents and young adults (and not only them), the emphasis appears to have shifted: the gender or sex of the partner becomes secondary— whether man, woman, nonbinary, trans—and what takes center stage is one's own self-definition ("Who am I?" "How do I name myself?), rather than "Who do I love?" In other words, the axis of the narrative no longer revolves around the object, but around the identity from which one desires, accompanied by a relative indifference toward the partner's traditional gender categories.

Several adolescent patients have been surprised and sometimes irritated while telling me about their romantic or sexual adventures. When I inquire about the gender of their partners, they regard it as totally irrelevant whether these experiences occur with a man or a woman. Below I share two brief clinical vignettes that illustrate this regressive shift in emphasis from the object to identity, and the generational sensitivity regarding gender language and ways of naming oneself.

Some years ago, my first adolescent patient who identified with the pronouns "they/them" was deeply offended when I asked about her partner's gender, replying irritably: "*Who cares?*" It is worth mentioning that that was our second and last session, as she stopped seeing me before we could even begin treatment, claiming I was too old for her—and it seems she was right. At the time, I struggled to understand that it might be of no importance to her, and I confess that even today, I haven't improved much in accepting the idea that the gender of the object someone chooses is not crucial to understand.

Another adolescent patient, who was biologically female, with very feminine features, who adopted the pronouns "he/ him", when I tried to explore what attracted her to being a man, she replied: "I don't want to be a man, I AM a man; I don't need an explanation for what I am" —although over time we were able to understand some reasons underpinning her identification with the male sex.

In contemporary discourse, the emphasis is not on the person with whom one maintains a romantic or sexual relationship, but on who one is: man, woman, both, neither. There is a search for identity without a desire for understanding.

As we know, for Freud, identification is primary and "object choice is based on the model of self-love." In other words: being precedes loving; identity comes first, and only later does object choice emerge. In "On Narcissism: An Introduction"

(1914), Freud writes that "from the beginning the individual carries with him a core of self-love" from which the capacity to love objects will later be constituted.

However, some contemporary approaches have proposed processes of becoming without stable identity anchors. From the psychoanalytic clinical perspective, however, it is essential to distinguish between the multiplicity of identifications characteristic of a developing and transforming ego and the absence of a sufficiently cohesive self. Subjectivity may indeed be fluid and plural, but it requires a psychic framework that enables continuity, differentiation, and a coherent sense of history.

That is to say, the capacity for becoming presupposes a subject capable of absorbing experience without fragmenting. When identity fails to form, anxieties of annihilation emerge, along with self/non-self-confusions, failures in symbolization, and archaic defenses. Conversely, denying identity does not free the subject; but rather exposes them to the disavowal of their most basic need: to exist as someone. We cannot deny that identity, narcissism, and the Oedipus Complex remain key concepts for understanding the psyche in psychoanalysis.

The contemporary viewpoints do not annul the Oedipus; but rather shifts the focus from the anatomical axis in order to situate it within the complex articulation between identity and culture. The Oedipus remains structuring; the need for a third remains as does the unavoidable acknowledgment of anatomical difference. Yet in a world of immediate satisfaction, in which everything seems possible thanks to new technologies and scientific advances, it becomes more difficult to accept what has been anatomically inherited, clinging to the illusion of being whoever one wishes or believes oneself to be.

Latin American psychoanalytic thought has made fundamental contributions to understanding this complexity, particularly by integrating the cultural, historical, and gender dimensions that traverse the Oedipal conflict. Leticia Glocer

Fiorini (2002, 2010) proposes an in-depth revision of the concept of sexual difference and the notion of gender identity. For her, subjectivity is constituted as a network of multiple, shifting identifications that are not reducible to the man/woman binary. From this perspective, the Oedipus complex remains a symbolic structure but ceases to be a closed model: it becomes a matrix to be read through cultural configurations and new forms of difference. Glocer Fiorini underscores that identity is not an essence but a position within the discourse and the desire of the Other, and that object choice does not define the subject's identity but expresses it in a transitory way.

Emilce Dio Bleichmar (1997, 2006) proposes that the constitution of the sexed subject is a process of symbolic and relational attribution that does not derive automatically from anatomy nor from a presumed symbolic "lack." In her view, sexual identity results from an "attribution of meaning and desire" through which culture and family inscribe differences. She stresses that a fundamental theoretical error has been the conflation of gender identity with object choice.

Her thinking therefore converges with the perspective developed here: identity is the structural basis of desire, not its consequence, reminding us that being and feeling precede object choice.

Along the same lines, Mariam Alizade (2007), the first chair of the IPA's Committee on Women and Psychoanalysis (COWAP), addresses femininity not as a destiny but as a subjective construct that articulates desire, pleasure, and symbolic power. Her reading of femininity highlights the role of aggression, rivalry, and autonomy, dismantling the classical notion of female passivity. Alizade notes that, in the analytic experience, women do not seek to complete a lack, but to elaborate their unique way of desiring within a symbolic fabric that does not always include her. This idea resonates with Kramer Richards's stance, which recognizes in her patients the need to reconstruct their place in the love scene without reducing it to an ideal derived from the norm.

Patricia Alkolombre—also a former COWAP chair——introduced (2015) the concept of "symbolic motherhoods" showing how the wish to be a mother—traditionally conceived by Freud as a substitute for the penis—is transformed in the current context. Today, many women choose not to have children or experience motherhood outside the heterosexual and biological model. This cultural shift, Alkolombre notes, requires a revision of the classical Oedipus, since the desire for a child as symbolic compensation for the lack of a penis has lost its relevance. Many women experience a sense of completeness oriented toward aspirations far removed from becoming mothers. We might consider that a re-orientation toward new forms of creativity and filiation is taking place.

Likewise, the Venezuelan psychoanalyst and writer Ana Teresa Torres (1998) has explored how cultural narratives shape female subjectivity. In her studies of narrative and psychoanalysis, Torres shows that myths, among them that of Oedipus, are not only psychic structures but also cultural devices of meaning that organize collective desire. In her reading, the female Oedipus cannot be understood without considering the discourses of power, morality, and gender that each era imposes. Although formulated nearly three decades ago, these ideas remain relevant to the current situation of new gender identities.

These authors converge on a central idea: female Oedipal experience is not resolved in anatomical difference nor in heterosexuality, but in the symbolic configuration of identity and in the diverse ways the subject appropriates her desire. They therefore coincide with Kramer Richards in that psychoanalytic theory must open itself to the plurality of subjective experiences without losing its clinical anchoring.

Other authors writing on gender diversities and the contemporary Oedipus argue that the emergence of trans, nonbinary, and fluid identities does not negate the Oedipus; rather, it reveals it as a symbolic, not anatomical, structure.

Judith Butler (1990, 2004), in *Gender Trouble*, proposes a performative theory of gender according to which the categories "man" and "woman" do not reflect an inner essence or biological truth, but are an effect produced by the repetition of acts and socially regulated meanings. From this perspective, identity does not emanate from the body nor is it an interior substance; it is constituted in relation to language, norms, and the desire of the Other. Consequently, there would be no gender identity "prior" to acts; on the contrary, acts (practices, modes of naming oneself, positions) are what progressively constitute identity in its becoming.

For his part, Ralph Roughton (2018) proposes that trans identities illustrate a variation of the Oedipal process and suggests understanding trans identities not as failures in Oedipal resolution, but as variants of the identificatory process.

Ken Corbett (2009) critiques the heterosexual normative ideal of classical theory. For him as well, masculinity and femininity are subjective projects.

These authors propose that the Oedipus does not determine gender; rather, it frames it as a symbolic problem, involving being someone in relation to another who also desires. Today identity operates in such a way that first I am someone and then I love someone—but unlike the classical model, "who I love" does not necessarily correspond to a specific gender. Whether or not we agree with these proposals, it is clear our theories must expand to account for new clinical modalities.

We can conclude that Kramer Richards's reading restores to the female Oedipus complex its clinical and structural complexity and enables its metapsychological updating. It is not a matter of abandoning the Oedipus, but of expanding it—extending it beyond anatomical determinism and reproductive teleology—to situate it as a symbolic matrix in which anatomy, identity, desire, and law are worked through under multiple configurations.

It no longer seems feasible to follow a linear or universal path of the Oedipus complex to account for the outcomes of sexual identification. Instead, we analyze the complexity of each individual case. Clinical listening precedes theory. This doesn't mean we underestimate importance of theory, but rather we are embracing it within a broader context that encompasses new variables.

In contemporary experience, marked by plural identities and evolving gender configurations, the central focus no longer orients to "who I love" as a sign of normality, but rather around "who I am" and from which place I desire. This does not dissolve the structure; it presupposes it. Clinical practice shows that Oedipal triangulation, the experience of exclusion, rivalry and the aspiration to be "the most loved" persist as core elements that are rewritten in each individual life.

The challenge for psychoanalysis is to sustain an expanded metapsychology capable of maintaining our roots while also accommodating differences and comprehending the dynamics of suffering and desire.

We, psychoanalysts are called upon to rethink the concept of Oedipus, given its enormous complexity, precisely so as not to relegate it to the background, but to keep it alive where it has always belonged: at the intersection of anatomy, identification, desire, love, rivalry, ambivalence, loss, and law, so that each person may find their own place in relation to their desire, the desire of the other, and their place in the world.

References

Abraham, N., & Torok, M. (2001 [1987]). *La cripta y el fantasma*. Buenos Aires: Amorrortu, pp. 113–143.

Alizade, M. (2007). La femineidad y el deseo. En *Revista de Psicoanálisis*, APA, Vol. LXIV (1), pp. 23–45.

Alkolombre, P. (2015). Maternidades simbólicas y filiación contemporánea. En *Estudios sobre la Mujer y Psicoanálisis*, IPA Papers, pp. 77–103.

Butler, J. (1990). *Gender Trouble: Feminism and the Subversion of Identity*. New York: Routledge, pp. 1–34 (ch. 1).

——— (2004). *Undoing Gender*. New York: Routledge, pp. 17–40.

Corbett, K. (2009). *Boyhoods: Rethinking Masculinities*. New Haven: Yale University Press, pp. 3–29.

Dio Bleichmar, E. (1997). *La sexualidad femenina y la teoría psicoanalítica*. Buenos Aires: Paidós, pp. 45–78.

——— (2006). *Nuevas perspectivas en psicoanálisis y género*. Madrid: Biblioteca Nueva, pp. 101–128.

Freud, S. (1905). Tres ensayos de teoría sexual. En *Obras Completas*, Amorrortu Editores, Tomo VII, pp. 109–224.

——— (1914). Introducción del narcisismo. En *Obras Completas*, Amorrortu Editores, Tomo XIV, pp. 65–98.

——— (1925). Algunas consecuencias psíquicas de la diferencia anatómica entre los sexos. En *Obras Completas*, Amorrortu Editores, Tomo XIX, pp. 275–286.

Glocer Fiorini, L. (2002). *El enigma de la feminidad: debates actuales*. Buenos Aires: Paidós, pp. 9–37.

——— (2010). *La diferencia sexual en debate*. Buenos Aires: Paidós, pp. 55–92.

Kaës, R. (2012). *Transmisión de la vida psíquica entre generaciones*. Buenos Aires: Amorrortu, pp. 21–64.

Roughton, R. (2018). Transgender identities and the Oedipal field. *Journal of the American Psychoanalytic Association*, 66(2), pp. 245–274.

Torres, A.T. (1998). *La herencia cultural y la subjetividad femenina*. Caracas: Monte Ávila Editores, pp. 15–62.

Responses of Arlene Kramer Richards To the Contributors

Arlene Kramer Richards

Hasidic Saying:

Why did God create the world?
Because he loves stories.

I love stories, conversations too. Especially conversation that includes stories. I thank all of the contributors to this controversial discussion for your erudition, willingness to engage, and especially for taking the clinical situation as the center of our work.

Response to Daniel Benveniste:

Thank you Daniel for your formidable research and logical thinking. I now see that the link between feeling and thinking is actually metaphor just as all language is metaphor. (Lakoff & Johnson, 2003).

The Oedipus story uses metaphor to embody a child's feelings of love, hate, jealousy and rivalry into a story that evokes childhood feelings. Evoking those feelings in an older person allows more effective ways of dealing with them than six-year-olds can muster. Thinking this way, we can understand the stories in many cultures as conveying what the social world wants of the individual and what the individual requires of the social world.

In many of the stories, copulation is both forbidding and productive. Feelings of love and the desire to be loved, even exclusively loved, are encapsulated in metaphor and transmitted to the social group as "just so" expressions of what is desirable and what is forbidden.

By tracing the reactions of young animals to adult mating behavior Benveniste shows how universal the action is in primates as well as humans of cultures far removed from Western European influence. The expressions of jealousy, rage, love and curiosity by the young are clear evidence that what Freud saw as the Oedipal story is not unique to Freud's ideas or Sophocles' play.

The appearance of curiosity, jealousy, rage, and love opens up the child's world to contradictory, complex and demanding thought. This kind of thought uses metaphor to reconcile the contradictions of love and hate that adult life will require of a child in any culture. this complexity and contradiction are the key problems of adolescence when a child transitions to adulthood.

Especially important is Benveniste's account of the male and female children's attempts to cope with the triad, keep exclusive control of the mother, and avoid enraging the father. That this is true for both boys and girls makes the work of understanding the way our patients negotiate their love lives and their sexual choices fascinating.

References

Lakoff, G. & Johnson, M. (2003). *Metaphors We Live By*. Chicago: U. Chicago Press

Response to Christina Biederman

I am grateful for Christina Biedermann's description of the line of thought about mothers and mothering. Surely motherhood and the capability to give birth and to nurture babies is a very powerful source of female experience. And the realities as well as the fantasies of motherhood are important to all people. But most women in our time spend most of our lives not in pregnancy, childbirth and nursing. What most women experience is a life of work inside and/or outside the home. Romance, pleasure and love are far larger in women's minds than the joys of childbirth and nursing. Many mothers experience their pregnancies as exhausting, many experience nausea, vomiting, back pain and fear of the coming birth.

After giving birth the sleepless nights, physical depletion of lactation, uncertainties about what to do about all the details of raising a child make huge demands on a mother. All over the planet women are choosing to have fewer children or none at all.

What do women really want? Freud's question resonates today. It is answered in pop music: Girls just want to have fun. I believe that young women today see themselves as wanting pleasure, wanting to be loved, wanting to be admired, wanting to be desired, wanting to experience their own desire and satisfaction of that desire. Yet apart from the French analytic literature very little attention is paid to these desires.

Boys too want fun; avoiding unpleasure and maximizing pleasure are universal. Whether cis gender or trans, whether heterosexual, bisexual or homosexual, we all crave pleasure. And the sexual organs are neurologically wired to be great source of pleasure. So, the avoidance of thinking, talking, theorizing, and writing about the satisfactions and deprivations of pleasure are, to my mind, the most important next step in our quest for understanding our patients as well as ourselves.

Response to Thomas DePrima

Thank you Dr. DePrima for extending the conversation to include a point of view that no longer restricts our thinking to the sexual binary or the nuclear family paradigm. In other words, for bringing our conversation into the contemporary world. As things seem now, development is no longer a straight (pun intended) path, nor is it predictable or continuous. I worry that analytic theory, derived almost entirely post facto and from pathology, is really relevant to the uncertainties and complexities of clinical practice.

Having worked in the past decade largely in China and having been told in no uncertain terms that I do not understand what is normal in their culture, Chinese analysands, supervises and students have taught me a lot about diversity.

For example, the practice of having children sleep with parents until well into latency is commonplace in China but seems an invitation to incest and child abuse in Western terms. Having children live for extended periods with grandparents or more distant relatives challenges my ideas of the need for continuity and consistency in living arrangements, despite my own experience of being cared for by grandparents and teen-age uncles. And the sense of parenting responsibilities and responsibilities of grown children to aging parents who may have taken little or no part in their children's upbringing does not match Western practices.

But the cultural differences also exist between different generations living in the same place because they have grown up in different times. Acceptance of trans people has been a recent challenge in Western culture that separates current teens and young adults from their parents just as acceptance of homosexual love has been and still is an issue between older and younger generations of people who are now middle aged and aged.

Differences like these can also separate therapist or analyst from patient. It takes work on the part of the therapist to understand such differences. It takes even more work to empathize with people whose mores differ from those of the therapist. It helps to have a cohort dealing with the same problems. So, I welcome being reminded of the tremendous changes in our own culture.

Response to Merle Molofsky

Merle Molofsky gives us a serious and comprehensive account of her experiences and her reading in the analytic theories about the female Oedipus. I appreciate her willingness to add to the literature I cited the work of Doris Bernstein.

Unfortunately, I do not agree with Bernstein's view that the little girl inevitably experiences her vulva as a void with no closure. Every little girl who has experienced toilet training knows that she has powerful muscles that can contain or withhold urination. She also has experienced the power of her sphincter muscles in defecating and in withholding defecation until she is in a suitable place for it.

According to Bernstein the little girl grows up believing herself to have an uncontrollable, indefensible hole in her body. Bernstein believed that this led to vagueness of thought and failure to master such thinking as that required for science, mathematics and philosophy. I do not agree that this is a realistic view of ordinary female development.

In ordinary toddler development autonomy and separation from the mothering person are central. A very key feature of the development of autonomy is the awareness of the power of one's own body, what Freud called the body ego. The individuation part of the separation-individuation line of development centers on the body ego.

For some girls this can be interfered with by intrusion. I many years ago treated a young woman who had been intruded upon in her early years by having her urinary tract stretched in an attempt to deal with her excessive withholding of urine and explosive release of it when pressure of the bladder forced its release. Her insistence on constant contact with her mother was seen as a separation problem by previous therapists. In the course of a stormy analysis, we found that she was passionately defending her autonomy by her insistence on dominating her mother.

The Oedipal aspect of this development had to do with having, like Electra, an absent father and a fear of the violence of men. Electra had a father who sacrificed her older sister to fulfill his own image of himself as a powerful man. Her mother Clytemnestra hated Electra's father for killing their daughter and Electra's older sister Iphigenia. So, Electra had reason to hate and fear her parents and the identifications with them that formed a dynamic part of herself. This is not a prototype of ordinary female development either. My point in the paper is that we need multiple perspectives to understand female development and that we cannot find a single prototypic story that covers all that happens in a girl's development into a woman. I thank Merle Molofsky for her important contribution to this conclusion.

Response to Adriana Prengler

Adriana Prengler opens up the theory of the Oedipus to a new level of understanding by emphasizing the contributions of Spanish and Latinx analysts to the deeper questions of identity and desire. Especially important to me is her understanding of the developmental status of identity as prior to the institution of desire.

While we have long known that children between 18 and 36 months can reliably indicate their connection understanding of themselves as like a girl doll or like a boy doll. This occurs before the 3–6-year Oedipal period.

Prengler is the first to use this observation and elaborate it into a clinical proposition. No one before Prengler to my knowledge has drawn the conclusion that identity formation precedes falling in love with another. The beautiful thing about this is that we share identity issues with all others. Both boys and girls work on understanding themselves before falling in love. Both can envy, both can hate, both can experience a variety of emotions. Rivalry and guilt are not exclusive to biological males; envy and shame are not the province of biological females.

Understanding our patients in this way frees us to follow their particular paths to the selves they construct and the way they love so that they can feel themselves authentic and acceptable to themselves and others. I am very grateful for Prengler's sophisticated, scholarly, and original response.

Conversations with Arlene Kramer Richards

M. Sagman Kayatekin

AKR During my years in College, I slowly realized that I had problems and that I was doing some things that were good for me and some that were self-defeating, and I knew then that I needed treatment. I got into a psychotherapy with someone whom my parents friends recommended. I had a few sessions with him because I was going back to school.

That was during the summer break of the first year in college, and he was really terrible. He was much dumber than I was, and he knew it, and I knew it, and that didn't work at all. For example, I came in wearing a white shirt that was tailored like a man's shirt, and he said to me, 'you have penis envy.' In the first session! As if he spoke to a five-year-old in a first interview and his evidence was that I was wearing this tailored white shirt.

MSK That's quite a 'deep' interpretation. Was he a psychoanalyst?

AKR He was rejected from New York Psychoanalytic. So, he was a psychotherapist of a kind, psychoanalyst of a maverick kind. He called himself a psychoanalyst, but he was someone who had not had full analytic training. I think he had gone to some courses. Whatever he was, he sure was someone who was very insecure about being dumb and yet I did get something out of it just talking to him. I learned some things about myself just from hearing myself talk, just as I am learning as I am talking to you.

MSK Yes.

AKR I think the method is so good that even someone who isn't good at it can do very good work sometimes. Anyways, I stuck with it till it was time to go back to school, and said, thank you very much, and left and did better from then on.

Later on I got into analysis with Arlow. It was during my own analysis that I got interested in becoming a psychoanalyst. I had known for many years that I was so depressed, and I had to work very hard to fight against the depression. I had to work all the time; I did so many things and the time had come when my husband was finishing his analysis so it looked like we might have enough money for me to start.

And the impetus finally came one day when I was crossing the street, and a big truck came to a screeching halt before hitting me. The truck driver leaned out of the window and said to me 'what's the matter with you lady, you're trying to get killed and it'll be my fault?'

So, he made a very serious interpretation, and I understood the seriousness of the situation. I was in graduate school at the time trying to work on my dissertation and I had very mixed emotions about finishing the dissertation and being able then to get a job in the academic world which I wanted. But I understood that if I got a job in the academic world it wasn't going to be in New York City. You don't start out that way, you start out at small college. But my husband was very involved in the New York Psychoanalytic and in his practice and he wasn't moving anywhere.

Thus, it seemed like I had to choose between an academic life and my family, and I chose my family but that made me very sad about finishing my dissertation and having nowhere to go after that.

MSK   In some ways you're analytic journey kind of starts in an interesting way because most people that I know who are in analytic training, are also doing psychotherapy and psychiatry and so forth. You're doing something very different as work, so that gives an interesting perspective. I would think eventually it could have been enriching because you have a foot outside of the potentially constraining, almost monochromatic life of working in psychotherapy and becoming a psychoanalyst. Most of the times our professional lives just consist of those very related and to a degree, narrow fields.

AKR   Yes and luckily enough I did take a few courses that were useful. One in this psychology of Piaget, who was himself analyzed although he wasn't an analyst and whose interest in how children learn fit in with my interest. That had developed in college; about how we know anything, about the philosophy of science, about how do we find things out. There were other thinkers about child psychology in particular who were thinking about how children learn, and this is related to how scientists learn. The development of curiosity, the development of skepticism, the development of becoming part of a community of learners. Interaction with people who have the same kinds of questions in mind so it fit together very well, except that I felt I still wasn't meeting my parents' expectations that I should be a woman whose husband supports her.

By now Arnie was a doctor, and he had gone through analytic training, I had completed my graduate studies and so I was very conflicted about continuing my career and how I wanted to do it. I knew Edith Jacobson and I called her and asked her if I could come in and see if I could become a patient and she said she was sorry but she didn't have any time. I was crushed. I couldn't think of another woman analyst who I knew. I wanted a woman analyst.

As a context, at that time my son was 12 years old, and he was preparing for his bar mitzvah. This had been a very difficult time for me because I felt he was like moving into the world of being a man and not my little boy anymore. And all the years that Arnie had been working so hard and his schooling and everything, I had become very close with Stephen. I really cared about him a lot and the thought that it was better for him not to be that close with me was very sad for me. It was sad because it resonated with the story of my life. I didn't understand this at the time, but it resonated with having left my poor little brother behind when I went off to university and I left him behind with my parents who I knew were not fit parents. I felt very guilty about the big turn approaching—here Stephen was going off to be a man.

Arnie told me that a Dr. Arlow who was at the New York Psychoanalytic had recently written a very good paper about bar mitzvah in which he understood some of this and maybe that would be the right person for me to approach next.

I read the paper. It made sense to me. It's a very nice paper and I went for an interview with Doctor Arlow, and I explained that I had wanted such help for a long time but couldn't afford to and was busy supporting my family. I was a schoolteacher and all that, and now I had enough money to have an analysis, and I certainly needed it because I understood this deep underlying depression was not good and was going to get me killed eventually if I kept up going on like this.

He said, how did you come to me, and I said, "Well my husband was a student of yours and he told me about this paper you wrote, and I read the paper, and it was very helpful, and I thought you could help me." He said, "Your husband? I don't remember your husband." I said, "You mean you want me to believe that when he said he was in class with you he was really out with a blonde?"

He got so embarrassed and of course he was being kosher. At that time, you weren't supposed to know anything about the analyst and here I am. I knew that he wrote this paper, and I had read it. He knew my husband, thought he was smart and kind, and all that.

MSK It wasn't working but he was trying to be "anonymous" right?

AKR Yes, exactly. Anyway, he agreed that I could work with him. There he said 'Well, I know him, but I just couldn't tell you. But you never let go of it.' We just thought it was very funny which it was; it was ridiculous, so I said some sort of affirming words, that I understood where he was coming from and it was just OK to see that he follows the party line. Except that it didn't work.

Initially the analysis about the theme of "How come you don't want to move to the suburbs with your children because you care about your children so much and why are you letting them live in the city?" It's the same stuff that my parents were telling me. Go be a housewife in the suburbs. But he was implying that

103

he was asking to understand why I didn't want that route. Though to me it sounded very similar to, in fact it sounded exactly like what my parents wanted me to do and were pressuring me on. He and they both were telling the children were not well taken care of because they were living in the city where it was dirty and it was crowded, and it was dangerous and why was I doing this to them? And neither my parents, nor Arlow, could accept that I wanted and needed to continue my career for intellectual reasons and because that was how I had found peace with myself and peace in the world.

I could do something good, and I needed to do something good, and I needed to work hard. This was important to me, so he didn't fully understand it either. It felt like he was not inviting us to a mutual curiosity where he was curious and I was curious.

Had I gone to live in the suburbs I would have become as depressed as my mother was in the suburbs. I mean I saw that my mother, when she stopped working, she became such a depressed person. I told him I was not wanting to be like that, and I knew I already was a depressed person so why add that to make things even worse? Forget it.

MSK I don't know how to say this properly, but you have a kind of very unique, rebellious streak right from the start. That's a very old side of you. That, I believe is what I am hearing as a theme of your life. Here you are disagreeing with Arlow right from the start.

AKR Yes, that's a very old side and I needed it to survive. Because of coming from feeling like being an orphan. My mom was not around for the whole week; she would visit for a dinner once a week on Fridays. And "being like an orphan" was a strong anxiety of mine.

MSK I'm also thinking about your primary femininity issue and this paper we're going to publish that is also a very old side of you. The way you perceive the world is not mainstream it's a person with deep curiosity, and creative kind of rebellious, something like that.

AKR Yes absolutely and that curiosity and creativity was encouraged by the experience at the University of Chicago that I started at the young age of 16. A place where students were taken very seriously. What you thought mattered, you know. I knew other people would listen to what you were saying. All of the teaching there at that time, it's not true anymore, but all of the teaching there was through seminars.

MSK I was amazed with what you told me about University of Chicago of those years. Sounds like the mythical Aristotelean Academia almost—where you learn to develop ideas with a small group of students and a highest quality scholar leading, facilitating and joining the discussions. It develops a deep sense of trust in your mind.

AKR Yes, this was a really amazing thing. And, yes, economically it's not viable now, but it was wonderful when it happened. This was a great experience of support for me it was so important that the college years were tremendously important, and it had been terrible to think that my parents did not want me to continue there. I mean it was absolutely awful for me that they didn't support it, and they didn't value it, and they didn't think I should be doing it.

You know, I've been thinking about how I got analytic training, as we talked about last time. I started by having an analysis, which I needed for personal reasons, not for training.

At the time that I started my analysis, I was working as a psychologist and doing well with that and enjoying it. I was at Columbia, doing statistics and research design and running this project, and I loved doing it. So, I had no intention of becoming a psychoanalyst at that time.

And then the money for research dried up, and my children graduated from elementary school, and I had no real reason to continue that job, the job was done and was done well. We made the pages of *The New York Times* with it, and we had a big influence on high schools all over the country. They did not have any interruptions.

MSK Do you still have that *NYT* page?

AKR Do I have it? No, but I could get it. And I was in analysis at the time, and I was talking about. I don't even remember what, in my analytic session, and suddenly my analyst said, you didn't read today's Times? which he had never said anything like that before, and then I discovered that our research was reported in *The New York Times*.

MSK Well, that's something, *The New York Times*.

AKR *The New York Times,* yes. And it had a tremendous impact. Many schools adapted the kind of the things that we recommended, and there were no high school disruptions, the way there were the college disruptions. Although most of the people who were to be drafted were the ones who graduated from high school and didn't go to college, because there was an exemption: If you were in college, you didn't have to serve in the army, yes. So, even though they were the ones most at risk, there was nothing in the way of demonstrations, when they used our model. I've had to negotiate with the students. So, we're very happy, very satisfied with that.

But then came a new administration and I had to choose from different alternatives. One, I had an offer from a university in the Southwest for a tenure-track job. That was impossible, because my family and everything was in New York. And my husband wasn't going to move to some place in the Southwest that didn't even have an analytic institute.

And the other choice was to go with the U.S. Office of Education and do a lot of traveling, and that was not a good thing either, to teach people how to do what we had done with our research, how to set up similar research designs. Well, I was not going to do that.

So, I decided I had been very interested in working with kids with learning disabilities, which I did before this research job. At that time, I had discovered, or I thought I discovered, that most of these kids, while they did have some neurological issues, they also had many and debilitating emotional issues around not feeling as good as others. Feeling disabled, feeling hopeless about themselves, feeling self-hatred. I was very interested in working on that and I opened a practice, and I was filled up pretty quickly.

And then a colleague called and said. "You know, we're getting together a group to study with Martin Bergmann to study psychoanalytic theory." I said, "oh, that's very interesting, I think I'll do that." It would give me more connection to this field, and it will be more support, because I was working quite alone.

So, I joined that group, and there were 8 guys and me. This was something I had experienced through graduate school as well, with doing the courses that the girls didn't want to do. And we decided that after all, after doing some reading and doing some discussing, that it would be wonderful to read Freud beginning to end, and the *Standard Edition* had just come out at that time.

107

MSK   24 volumes?

AKR   Well, the 24th volume had just come out, yes. We decided to hire George Gross, who was then at New York Psychoanalytic, and ask him if he would like to read through all of Freud with us, and he was delighted. He thought that was a great idea, and we did that. It took us three and a half years to do it, meeting once a week. And that was so interesting, and it seemed to me to illuminate much of what I was experiencing in my child psychotherapy practice, which is what it turned out to be. In time, the members of the group got more interested. We would add a second evening of the week, and we would hire everyone who taught at New York Psychoanalytic to give us the same course, except we'd pay for it. They were not paid for teaching, and they already had the course outline and all the readings and everything, and they didn't have that much more work to do, to do the same thing for us. And at this time, of course, they were paid. They would be doing something illegal, if they would supervise us, so they couldn't supervise us, but they could teach us the same courses they were teaching.

I was working a lot with adolescents. Because that was the most difficult work and everyone didn't want to do it. And so, I got a lot of referrals for adolescents. And adolescent children of colleagues, actually, so they were very psychologically minded.

I met a man named Donald Kaplan, who was at the time, organizing the New York Freudian Society. And I asked him to be my supervisor. He was a psychologist. I was referred an analytic case, and I started working with Kaplan. And all this was going on, and then, I needed a second supervisor, so I got a second case.

Norbert Friedman, who was at IPTAR, was highly regarded as a supervisor, so I had him as a supervisor. So, I was in supervision twice a week, and I had two, five-time-a-week cases. I was launched on an analytic career through this circuitous way. And I loved doing it, and I was good, so my patients stayed and got better, and they were really very gratifying days.

Two or three years later Donald Kaplan called me up one day and said, "Look, I'm running for president of the New York Freudian Society, and I need votes. Would you join the society and vote for me?" I felt very grateful to him for the good supervision I had gotten. I said, yes, I'd be glad to do that. A week later, Norbert Friedman called me up and said, "I hear you're joining the Freudian Society. Didn't you learn from me? Aren't you interested in IPTAR?" I joined IPTAR, too. So, I became very involved in psychoanalytic politics in a weird, weird way.

Meanwhile, while studying with this group we read something in Freud in the Standard Edition, that said 'Women don't have genital anxiety because they don't have a genital to lose'. And I said, "That's not right! I have a genital. Not like yours, but I have one. And it gives me pleasure. And I would be really worried if anyone tried to hurt it. Or hurt me by hurting it."

And this was how I started on a paper about female genital anxiety. And I was good friends with Charlie Brenner. We used to have lunch, a whole luncheon group he had every Friday. And I talked to him about it, and I said, you know, you wrote in your book, your big book, a whole chapter about why women are depressed because they think they've already lost their genital. And I said, "I don't think so, not from the women in my practice. And not from my own experience. I think that women value genital experience, and that genital experience starts very early, in little girl babies. I observed this in young children I cared for. I have diapered them; I don't know how many times. And they always love it. They love to be washed there, they love the experience of their genital, and I don't think they think it's been cut off. They enjoy it." And Charlie said, "Get the data and write the paper."

MSK Oh!?. That's interesting. It doesn't fit with the mythological image of Brenner who is a sharp critique of ideas that do not fit with his point of view.

AKR Remarkably generous of him. He welcomed talking about what he did not know just as much about what he knew.

MSK Oh, okay. That surprises me. Now, let me ask you a question. So, at this point in time, there's IPTAR, New York Freudian. But you're still outside of the mainstream of American Psychoanalytic? So, your institutes said, "Okay, we don't have to be a part of APSA, we can develop our institutes, if you like it or not, we're going to do it," something like that.

AKR Correct. These institutes were started originally by refugees from Europe who were analysts, and who were, for various reasons, unable to get along with the American establishment, and therefore, they got kicked out of New York Psychoanalytic, or what was then called Downstate, or what was then Columbia. They were not able to be subservient in the way they needed to be. They came in with the backing of their historical ties "Well, we know everything, we're Europeans, we were analyzed by Freud himself, etc. You know that Freud thought Americans were dumb and would be in psychoanalysis.

And there were also, a limited number of patients, and people were afraid to lose their patients to these other guys. And therefore, there was this animosity between them. So, the Europeans were willing to teach psychologists, because Freud said it's okay.

MSK How does all of this make sense?

AKR We're all member institutes of the American.

MSK But they're mostly white male Americans.

AKR Yes.

MSK And is there also anti-Semitism in this?

AKR No.

MSK Oh, Okay, so it's not anti-Semitic. It is "first come first served. I was here before, so sorry, not in New York, you go west," whatever, something like that. Territorial.

AKR Yes. They were just coming out of the Depression. They had all these people who were drafted, coming back. And there was a whole fear that there would not be enough patients. Some of the Europeans came just before the war, which meant just after the Depression, when everyone was terrified, I'm not going to be able to make a living. And some of them came after the war. When there was this fear of all the GIs coming back.

MSK The reason I'm asking is I know there is a period of anti-Semitism, early to mid-century, in academia.

AKR Oh, yes. Very much, Arnie talks about this. Wasn't true in Psychoanalysis though. Very different. But let me go back to the idea of castration and discussion with Freud and Brenner. So, I gathered the data and wrote the paper. I was surprised as you were just now. I was so surprised when he was so encouraging, I was just as astounded as I could be.

111

Oh, it took a lot of courage to say it to him in the first place, and then, to be encouraged. Oh my god!

MSK Yes, that's true. Maybe he liked that.

AKR Yes. Well, that's why I was thinking about it, because I was thinking about it going in with that paper.

So, Psychoanalytic politics. I got involved really very, early on. There were encouraging responses from colleagues about becoming involved in the larger psychoanalytic world. In the IPA, if not in the American. And we started Division 39 of the American Psychological Association. Division 39 was the psychoanalytic group. I organized the Mexican meeting, which was, like, the third meeting of that group, where we went to a destination, and talked about psychoanalytic issues, and read papers, and did a miniature version of what the American did at its meetings. We were imitating what the American did.

Because we thought it was a very good thing to have this cross-fertilization of different groups that would have their own ideas, and so there were some groups in LA, there were some groups in San Francisco, and of course, the New York groups. Then there was one in Florida, in Miami. All of these different groups of psychologists who had been trained by the European analysts. So wherever there were a large enough group of the European analysts, psychologists got trained.

Many of us felt that the training of psychologists was very important and should go on everywhere that the American Psychoanalytic had groups, had institutes. Why couldn't psychologists get analytic training in Chicago, in Detroit, in Cincinnati, all these places that the American had institutes when there were psychologists interested in doing this and willing to, you know, go through the years of training?

There was a group of people, not me, but a group of psychologists, started conversations with the American about doing this. With the idea that in these other places, there were not enough analysts. And there would be if they trained psychologists. There were four years of meetings. And then the American Psychological Association, the larger group, which was very big, I mean, it's 20,000 people at that time, it's more now, we invited the president and some other members of the American Psychoanalytic to Washington to discuss this issue. And they came.

A guy named Ed Joseph was the president of the American Psychoanalytic at the time. And he said, okay, you're inviting us, that means you'll pay, right? For the American Psychological, for that group, it was a small amount of money. It was ridiculous to argue about it, so they said, yes, we'll pay for your transportation and your hotel and your meals and everything, and we'll treat you to this meeting.

So, he came to the meeting, and said, "We have to think about it some more, we have to talk about it." Anyway, he deferred again. This was now the fifth year of such meetings. He deferred making any commitments. And he went back home to New York, and he sent the American Psychological Association his bill for his transportation for his hotel. And while he was at the hotel, he also brought his wife, so she had to be paid for as well. And...they brought a lot of personal laundry from home. They got the hotel to do their laundry. And he sent that bill with it!

MSK That's... that's really cheap I must say.

AKR After this, we were done. American Psychological Association said "Ed, here's your money, don't bother us ever again. We're not interested in talking to you ever again."

113

MSK This is a guy who's probably making enough money to have an apartment on the Fifth Avenue or something, right?

AKR Yes! Yes! It was totally a slap in the face. It was, you know a 'gotcha' for everything. I'll get you, talk to you, and I'll show you who's the boss.

The Mexican meeting of Division 39 was soon after this. I organized it and I was the program chair for that. We talked about joining the American Psychoanalytic, or the IPA, or whatever else we wanted to join. What should we do next? That was the central question. APA, our big organization said they want nothing more to do with these APSA guys. What do we do now?

Then came the idea that we sue them. We sue the American, for restraint of trade. That they have no scientific or philosophical reason for not training psychologists. It's just not wanting the competition from psychologists. In fact, Freud quite forcefully stated that medical training is irrelevant to becoming a psychoanalyst, and they had what they called in those days lay analysts which was psychologists, social workers, teachers, like Anna Freud. I mean, Freud was saying this about his own daughter. She's just as good as any other analyst, he was saying.

MSK This was more of an American issue, not true for Britain?

AKR Not true for Britain, not true for any place else in the world, only in the U.S. The French trained psychologists, the Spanish trained psychologists, the Argentinians, everybody, except the U.S.

MSK And it was not an IPA rule.

AKR No, but the American had a special position in the IPA. It's now lost, but as long as the American met IPA standards, they were able to put in some standards of their own. In fact, they were stricter standards than the IPA. In other words, if in the IPA you could train anybody, in the U.S, you could only train psychiatrists who had been to medical school and done a psychiatry residency. So, this special agreement meant that psychologists from the U.S. could not join the IPA.

Because in the U.S, only the American could set the standards. And the IPA agreed to this because, at the time, the IPA was very broke, and everyone in Europe was very, very poor. It was just after the Second World War. The Americans were supporting the IPA. The dues from the U.S. were perhaps 80% of their budget.

And they the Americans said, we'll pull out. We don't have to be members of the IPA if you don't agree to this. So, the IPA agreed. All of this I had learned from Martin Bergmann and other people who were involved at that time in trying to become psychoanalysts when they were "only" psychologists. They were not MDs.

So, we hired a lawyer who was a psychologist who was getting psychoanalytic training. Because the American had a rule that you could train psychologists or other people if they promise never to practice. So, they were going to get training and never practice. Well, forget that, of course. Everybody who signed that knew that it was not going to happen. That, of course, they were going to go into practice. What else? I mean, why else would they want analytic training from the American?

MSK Yes, there's a limit to human masochism, right?

AKR Yes. The idea was they would do research. They were allowed to do research. Or they were a professor of French, they were allowed to teach French literature from a psychoanalytic point of view, or whatever. I mean, all these ideas. But they practiced, they liked the practice, and they went on to practice on their own, afterward. It was a fake thing. Really just a fake thing.

And it was because institutes were not getting enough MDs to train, because MDs, in the US, at least had to pay very high fees for medical school, very high fees, and then had to work for very, very low salaries as interns and residents. So, everybody was in debt by the time they finished psychiatry residency and they really couldn't afford to do analytic training or analytic work.

It took years to get the American to agree to negotiate, and then there was many years of negotiation that led to nothing. So, it was really a long process.

MSK Yes, then came the laundry list, right?

AKR The "laundry" did it. That was the turning point. And so, this lawyer said, "It's clearly an economic issue. What we have to sue about is not what Freud said, or what science there was. What we have to sue about is they are protecting high fees." And one of the stupid things that Ed Joseph did was to say, "We can't let them in, they're going to have all these women psychologists, and they had very cheap training, and they're going to be able to work for low fee, and they're going to ruin it for everybody."

MSK You know, these guys who have autocratic tendencies occasionally say things that they should never have said. They get caught red handed.

AKR Yes. They should never have said it. It was the truth. But they shouldn't have said it. And once they said it, it was the last nail on the coffin. Then we won the lawsuit. During this process, suddenly, all of Arnie's colleagues and friends at New York Psychoanalytic who used to invite us to dinner parties, they would come to our house for dinner, kids would play together, all kinds of things, social interactions stopped.

MSK Oh.

AKR Because he was married to me. You don't fraternize with the enemy.

MSK Oh, he did even worse, you know, he married the enemy. That's when the idiotic comment was made where they suggested "You should divorce," right?

AKR Yes, or you are in trouble.

MSK I mean, it is unbelievable. It's somewhat absurd and almost funny now, but at the time, it's not funny. At that moment, some people took it very seriously.

AKR Yes! It was really so disappointing that they behave this way. I really thought they were friends. I got more involved in psychoanalytic politics than I wanted to be.

MSK By the time this lawsuit was in full force, you were now full-time practicing. You were in psychoanalytic world, in it.

AKR Yes, I was practicing psychoanalysis. And I was not charging low fees, which made them very angry. I had a sliding scale, I saw poor people for next to nothing, and I had some rich patients who really paid well.

MSK So it's a great statement that you don't need to have a penis, neither an anatomical nor a medical, 'MD penis' to do this. You must have been a real pain for a lot of people.

AKR Oh, yes. Absolutely. I remember one time, somewhat later on, after I had written this paper, Charlie Brenner invited me to a case conference that he ran at New York Psychoanalytic, to present a case. And I presented the case. It was a very interesting case of a young woman who had, at that time, lived in California. She was the daughter of a movie director. And she read this paper, and she said, "I need to have this person be my analyst." And she came to New York. We talked a little, and she got an apartment, she got a job! And she became an analytic patient.

So, one of the people in this seminar said. "But of course, you saw her at a low fee, right?" And I said, "well, actually no. Her family was willing to pay a fee commensurate with their economic status." And he said, "Oh, so the father was this famous director. And that's why they had the money." I said, "No, actually, the mother had the money. The father made a nice living, but the mother was the daughter of an English lord who had married this American guy, and she came with a nice estate." And they really got so angry.

You know, they were looking for all different ways to say that women don't have it, women are dependent, women are this and that. They would not focus on what the patient said and did, and what I said and did in the sessions. They kept drawing it into this political, economic thing. Which had nothing to do with what this patient was about.

MSK Why that stereotype, you think? I mean, because you and I talked about your Polish background, the mill owner grand Tante, and her daughter, your very close dear Tante, all working women and a culture where working women was praised.

AKR These analysts, many of whom were Jewish, but they were, second, third, fourth generation Americans, and they were so imbued in American culture. And they had nothing to do with this shtetl culture that my parents came from.

MSK So, an essential aspect of Americanization is the image where the wife stays at home, takes Mama's little helper, and so forth.

AKR Yes. And waits for the husband.

MSK They're used to that. They don't know the Eastern European culture.

AKR Exactly.

MSK It's an acculturation that happened in this country.

AKR Yes. And, and it was intentional. In building the country, you were not allowed to speak a foreign language. You know, the linguist joke about "trilingual, bilingual and American." That was absolutely intentional. It has changed now. Spanish is the second language of the whole United States now.

MSK Very interesting. Because if you look at Freud, it's a more along the lines of husband working, wife taking care of children, etc.

AKR Yes, when they became more assimilated in the Austrian culture. It was also wife at home. Austrian culture was Catholic. Very different. Very different.

MSK And a number of Eastern European, very prominent Jewish names that I know quite a bit about, like Karl Marx and Freud were Germanized. Well, the parents of Karl Marx had already converted, and the love of his life was a Christian German aristocrat, Jenny Von Westphalen. And then Freud was, at some points, ambivalent about his cultural identity, it seems.

AKR Yes, absolutely.

MSK There's something… They aren't like the Arnie you saw in Chicago. A practicing Orthodox, praying and following kosher, very much embedded in his traditional cultural identity.

AKR Well, that Arnie I saw in Chicago, was closer to the culture that my parents who came from came from Europe. He also thought of women as working. He also you know, so for me, he was the right guy. In the modern world working woman is generally more accepted now, despite the strong trends to revert that. But it wasn't the case in New York of my youth.

MSK So that was one of your political struggles. Egalitarianism of men and women. In psychoanalysis and other fields, and so forth.

AKR Yes. And that had a big influence on my analytic thinking as well. And that was why that young woman wanted to come all the way cross-country for her analysis.

MSK Yes, that's something.

AKR Yes. And why her family was willing to support that long analysis, and they didn't waver. They supported it the whole time. I mean, not just financially.

MSK Well it seems we diverged in a wonderful way. But for the purposes of these conversations, let me take us back to your analytic career. I mean, one fascinating thing I'm hearing is you actually were not too invested in becoming an analyst, and that probably made your analysis with Arlow more, for lack of a better word, neutral, or free. Because you didn't want to impress him to be an analyst and so forth. It was just, for your personal needs, your own curiosity and when you felt like it, you didn't hesitate to give it to him. Pretty straightforward.

AKR Yes, absolutely. I was not the easiest patient at all.

MSK Because, you know, in training analyses, people get a little stiff. And allowing the unfolding of a tasty negative transference is not that easy. So, that may have served you in a very interesting way.

AKR I think so. I think so. Let me tell you about my analyst's response to my papers, presentations on these issues.

I think it's very interesting, at least it was interesting to me, that when I wrote the first paper, Challenging the idea. I sent a copy to my analyst, it was after my analysis, and I sent him a copy, saying 'What do you think of this? Would you please correct where I'm wrong or question where I'm questionable."

And he wrote me back. Single space typed on a type-writer, that's what he used in those days, 10 pages. In which he said, basically, "You can't say something this controversial, without a lot more evidence, get a lot more evidence. It's not for a journal; it's probably for a book." In other words, he was saying, take more time, do more, do more, don't... let anyone see this. And I was surprised that he was, what seemed to me, quite timid.

MSK Mm.

AKR So, I sent it anyway. I sent it to the *International Journal.* It was the paper about female perversion. A telephone perversion in a woman. And that got accepted and there was not much controversy about it. I had given it orally at different places, including New York Psychoanalytic, and there was not that much controversy about it. It seemed that what I was calling a perversion, other people felt comfortable calling separation anxiety. Which was nice, and not sexy, and not demeaning, or anything like that.

And the whole point of the paper, was that it was nasty, that she was imprisoning her mother in this way. And that she was using her pain as a way to manipulate and control other people and her world. And a good friend of mine got it. She got the idea, and she said, "You know? Masochist is the leader." And she gave me a paper she had written previously, about how saying, "I'm in pain," manipulates the other person.

We were on the same wavelength. We were understanding female masochism in the same way. And this encouraged me a lot to then go on and write about female sexuality in a way that if not challenging, was at least different from what Freud was saying. And from what, particularly, the ego psychologists were saying. So, I was coming at it from the point of view of my own experience. And the experience of other women, who talked to me about their experience of their daughter's sexuality, of infantile sexuality in girls.

And they all said, the same thing. Girls are easy to toilet train. They like it. Boys are much harder. That's because the urine as it comes out, excites the labia and the clitoris. It is pleasurable to the little girl. Little girls smile when you diaper them. And sometimes giggle, that this is fun. And I went back and read Freud. And Freud's idea was that the little girl is a little boy until she sees a boy with a penis. In other words, she's satisfied with her own sexual equipment. To begin with.

MSK Freud has the theory that the little girl is a boy until she sees the boy?

AKR Yes!

MSK Oh, okay.

AKR Yes. But why call that being a boy? Why not call that being a little girl who can experience pleasure? Because he was thinking only a boy can have pleasure. Only the penis gives pleasure. What did he know? He never had a clitoris. And being very intellectual and visual and developed, he wasn't thinking about the knowledge and the experience of the psychomotor body, of the whole body. He was thinking of the eye. He learned through the eye, he read, he saw. This was very important.

MSK That's very interesting. Let me add to that, I'd never thought of that. He was a very prominent neuropathologist, do you know?

AKR Yes, yes!

MSK He did a lot of research on eels, so he used to draw them and so forth. He was very, very high class.

AKR Yes. And those eels... Changed from boy to girl.

MSK I didn't know that one.

AKR Yes! That's what was so fascinating about eels.

MSK That's really good.

AKR Research was done on eels, because their sexuality could change, and did.

MSK I missed that connection, okay. Maybe purposefully.

AKR Maybe purposefully. It's a very exciting idea. So, his mental furniture was such that this was a logical idea. On the other hand, my mental furniture came from learning theory, and largely from Piaget who talked about the kind of learning that comes from doing. Muscle learning, sensory learning.

MSK That's very interesting.

AKR From the experience of the body, pre-verbal, and verbal. Piaget's ideas really covered learning from age 1 to 6 to the same period that Freudians think, we all think, is so important in development, and lays down the basis for further mental life, for the rest of the person's life. So, this kind of learning, that you shouldn't turn this, you shouldn't touch the stove because it's hot, learning that if you put your thumb in your mouth, it's comforting. This kind of learning is the infant's tool to live in the world. And this kind of learning includes which parts of the body can be painful. And which parts of the body can give pleasure. And we know that the greatest nerve concentration in the whole body is not the eye or the ear or the tongue, but the clitoris.

MSK Hmm.

AKR More nerve endings there than anywhere else. So, a little girl learns very quickly that that's pleasurable, and that that can be very painful. Both. That if you hurt the clitoris, it really hurts. And if you touch it gently, that's fun!

MSK That's very interesting. So then, that maybe have some connection to the female circumcision.

AKR Yes, exactly. That is where female sexuality is located, and if you want to destroy female sexuality, destroy that part of the body.

MSK Hmm. I see. The other thing, though, is it's not too easy to visualize, unlike the boy's penis. Right?

AKR No! If you look down and spread your legs, you can see the whole thing. And you spread your legs every time you pee. All you have to do is look down, you see it.

MSK That's amazing. Little girls can recognize it early on, visually, too then.

AKR All they have to do is look! But you quickly learned that you're not supposed to look. That you're not supposed to be interested. That people get very upset if you're interested.

MSK Oh, that's very interesting because then the reverse is probably true for the boys. You better look and pee far away as much as you can. There are competitions around that.

AKR Yes.

MSK Oh, I see. So, shame is located into looking.

AKR Very quickly. Don't look at that, pretend you don't know, pretend you don't see, pretend you don't feel. Every little girl is taught that.

MSK I got you.

AKR Yeah. So, a very important paper. about that is called Everybody Must Be Just Like Me, by Elizabeth Lloyd Mayer, influenced me a lot to think about that. In her paper, she talked about her daughter, she had two daughters, so she was one of these women who had daughters and could observe early female development. Well, she had taught her daughter to look at herself and see it. It was okay, and she should be proud of it, and it was a good thing, and she had a nice experience of it. And when her daughter saw her father in the shower...

Oh, and the important thing I'm leaving out is that little girls are not taught the name of it. Little boys are taught it's a penis, but little girls are not taught that's a vulva.

And you have a vulva. But during the 60's–70's feminism, little girls were being taught, that's your vulva. Her daughter saw her father in the shower, saw his penis and said, Mommy! Daddy has something hanging from his vulva. So, the culture, of the feminist culture of that time, which encouraged women to even use a mirror to look down.

MSK Hmm.

AKR It really showed that if you didn't make them ashamed of it, girls could be very happy with having their sexual organ as it was. And not see the penis as something better but see the penis as something strange and different from what I have.

MSK Let me tell you a funny story. I know a little girl and she used to say, "boys have a tail."

AKR Yes! Yes

MSK Tail. What a degrading image to male grandiosity!

AKR Hangs down there like a tail. And it can lift up like a tail. She's absolutely right, it's a tail.

It had a real effect on me, and I think on many other women. And on psychoanalytic theory. I was just going one step further and providing the clinical material that went with that, with the idea that science is about building. We build on each other's work. We learn from each other, and we teach each other. And I thought Freud was perfectly right when he said, I don't understand women, it'll take women analysts to figure it out.

Psychoanalytic History—Sketches
The Power of Exclusion
(An Ode to Sheldon Bach and Sándor Ferenczi)

Carolyn Ellman

Previously published: Ellman, C. S. (2023). The power of exclusion (an ode to Sheldon Bach and Sandor Ferenczi). Psychoanalytic Psychology, 40(1), 43–49.

This paper is a tribute to my teacher, supervisor and mentor Sheldon Bach who would have been so happy to have heard me present this paper in 2021. Since Bach was one of the few analysts giving Ferenczi some of the recognition he deserved by calling him one of his "great influences on his thinking" (Bach, 2016, pp. xxvi) this would have given him such pleasure to see this tribute in print.[1]

Trying to follow the journey that started with my first conference in 1996 at NYU (where 365 people attended) and led to a book in 1998 called *The Modern Freudians* (Ellman, C. S., 1998), I have been trying to

---

[1]An earlier version of this paper was given by Carolyn Ellman as the annual Bert Freedman Memorial Lecture on November 7, 2021, at the Institute for Psychoanalytic Research and Training

make sense of what it means to be a Contemporary Freudian. The original conference covered many areas of technique, and I found it interesting in writing this paper to look back at what I thought Freudian psychoanalysis looked like in 1996. I wrote at the time: "The importance of the relationship to the analyst has been stressed by Freudians for years (Greenson, 1965, Loewald, 1960, Stone 1961). What is new is how much it is being stressed, how much or how little one concentrates on surface versus unconscious material, and how important are intrapsychic conflicts versus the emerging transference-countertransference dialogues (with a particular focus on the analyst's inner life, (p. xiii).

I also quoted Freud:

"Psychoanalysis is not, like philosophies, a system starting out from a few sharply defined basic concepts, seeking to grasp the whole universe with the help of these and, once it is completed, having no room for fresh discoveries or better understanding. On the contrary, it keeps close to the facts in the field of study, seeks to solve the immediate problems of observation, gropes its way forward by the help of experience, is always incomplete and always is ready to correct or modify its theories (Freud, 1923, p. 253).

By the time I worked on the *New Freudian Synthesis* (15 years after *The Modern Freudians*), we had the task of trying to understand not only the new role of the analyst but how much our colleagues were influenced by Klein, Winnicott, Bion and others and yet still called themselves Freudian. We asked them, what still makes you a Freudian?

Having lived through many changes in how we look at ourselves, it was only when I started reading Ferenczi with my Freud reading group in 2017, that I realized something that had been bothering me for many years. It was what I was grappling with in these two books: the strange disconnect between theory and technique. I didn't know at the time that Ferenczi was already thinking this way when he and Rank wrote their book on technique (Ferenczi and Rank, 1925). I knew in 1966 during my internship at Montefiore Hospital (a hotbed of New York Psychoanalytic analysts at the time) that the way my supervisor Sheldon Bach thought about patients had nothing to do with what they were teaching at Grand Rounds.

I didn't know Shelly was the type of clinician that Ferenczi was (Bach, 2000). He listened so intensely to the patient's experience and tried to enter their world and understand why they might have difficulty relating (whether it was due to early trauma and narcissistic problems). His approach wasn't dictated by theory alone. But when my study group started reading the Freud-Ferenczi correspondence I think that every one of us (6 people besides myself who had been studying together for 25 years) had the same distorted notions that had been perpetrated for years. Even though we had read Ferenczi's 1913 paper on "Stages in the development of the sense of reality" in our training as Freudians, we knew very little about him as a clinician. In fact, we had some notion that he was quite disturbed because he had an affair with his patient Elma who was the daughter of his mistress Gisella. We thought that he slept with many patients, and we thought that he had an infantile attachment to Freud. We thought that Freud turned his back on him because he slept with patients. It turned out that very little of this (other than the affair) was historically true.

GG1

I would like to go over some of the actual facts of the case before I put forth some hypotheses about why I think the Freudians turned their back on Ferenczi after he died in 1933 and why the contemporary Freudians did the same thing in the 1980s when the *Clinical Diary* was published and then the correspondence in the 1990s. Balint said that the fight between Freud and Ferenczi was one of the great tragedies of psychoanalysis because many people felt Ferenczi was one of the most important figures in the movement (Balint, 1968, p. 152). His patients included Ernest Jones, Melanie Klein, John Richman, Franz Alexander, Sandor Rado, Géza Róheim, Clara Thompson, Margaret Mahler, René Spitz, Alice and Michael Balint, Otto Rank and Sandor Lorenz.

GG2

He influenced object relations theory through the work of the Balints, Klein, and Winnicott. He influenced the interpersonal tradition through Fromm and Thompson, self-psychology, Lacanian theory and more. Many of his analysands started institutes in the U.S. Ferenczi was considered by his colleagues to be one of the best analysts of his time and everyone was sent to him including the most difficult patients; thereby, his influence affected the whole field (Aron and Harris, 1993). However, after his death hardly anyone (with a few exceptions) mentioned his work for over 50 years. The lack of attention, malicious rumors, active silencing and deliberate repression of Ferenczi's work—and other non-desirable early participants in Freud's circle—was called Totschweigen, "death by silence" by Esther Menaker (Rachman, 2017).

GG3

In reading the history of the conflict between Freud and Ferenczi, it is important to understand correctly why Freud was so upset with the contents of Ferenczi's paper on the "Confusion of tongues" (Ferenczi, 1933) and why this led to such an extreme disruption to their relationship. It is particularly important to make it clear to people that don't know the history of their relationship, that their falling out had nothing to do with his affair with his patient (which happened in 1911 and Ferenczi had been married to Gisella since 1919). Nor did it have to do with Ferenczi not accepting the presidency of the International Psychoanalytic Association in his later years, which Ferenczi had helped form in 1910 and which he was the president from 1918 to 1920. Freud, after he had been diagnosed with cancer in 1923, gave the mantle over to Rank and Ferenczi to work on technique (see Ferenczi & Rank, 1924). He said he had total trust in Ferenczi's ability with patients. In fact, he encouraged Ferenczi to try various techniques such as cutting the analysis short (following some ideas of Rank related to birth trauma) and then his relaxation techniques (Haynal, 1989). Freud was upset however when Clara Thompson told him that she had kissed Ferenczi; he worried that Ferenczi's relaxation techniques could go too far, and he wrote him in 1931 the so called "kissing letter" (Falzeder, 2000). This deeply hurt Ferenczi who felt that the Thompson episode had been contrived by Thompson out of jealousy for his patient RN and was upset that Freud didn't trust him more.

GG 4

Even though no one condones what happened with Ferenczi and Elma, I think it is important to know that Ferenczi had already brought up to Freud in 1910 that he needed more analysis and couldn't do it himself (Lugrin, 2021). He was a very big advocate for a long analysis for people practicing psychoanalysis. Ferenczi was convinced that his psychosomatic problems were related to his love life. He had been having an affair for many years with Gisella, an older woman who was married and whose husband wouldn't give her a divorce. She had two daughters and one of them, Elma, got very depressed. Her mother suggested that Elma see Ferenczi. In the history of this tragic story, one should understand that when Ferenczi realized he was falling in love with Elma, he asked Freud to see her since he knew he couldn't analyze her anymore. To add to this, when Freud had met Ferenczi in 1908 he was so taken with this young man that he had wanted Ferenczi to meet one of his own daughters (Haynal, 1992). Ferenczi's wish for analysis with Freud was about his confusion about Gisella and Elma with Freud having very complex feelings about Ferenczi wanting him as his analyst. He wanted Ferenczi to get on with his life and lead the psychoanalytic movement. It is not clear in reading about the analysis that Freud finally consented to, which was off and on during the war years between 1914 and 1916, how much of Ferenczi's desperation was about Elma and how much about his conflict of wanting love and admiration from Freud while at the same time wanting to separate from him [For clarification see Dupont, 1994]. However, if you read Yves Lugrin's 2021 book *Ferenczi on Freud's Couch* and you read about the torture Ferenczi felt about his love life, this was not a man who just "slept with patients."

GG 5

The other point that needs to be clarified is about mutuality. It is often stated that Ferenczi was the first analyst to understand the importance of a two-person mutually open relationship between patient and analyst and therefore the mother of relational therapy. In point of fact, Ferenczi did believe in honesty and trust as crucial to the analytic relationship (especially with traumatized patients) but his experiment with actual mutual analysis with his patient RN was very much against his will. He fought her for one year before he gave into mutual analysis and after a year of trying it he stopped it (much to her dismay) since he realized how much it was interfering with his other patients (many of whom like Thompson were jealous) and he couldn't be totally honest without betraying his other patients. He also realized his patients could hide behind mutual analysis and not stay focused on themselves. More than anything, Ferenczi was looking for honesty in the relationship and, like Winnicott later on, Ferenczi was willing to try many techniques to reach very traumatized patients.

So, what happened when Ferenczi wrote in 1932 the "Confusion of tongues" paper and wanted to present it to the 12th International Psychoanalytical Congress in Wiesbaden, Germany that year? What was in that paper that led to a break between two very close friends and collaborators, especially since a few years before in January 1928 Freud had written to Ferenczi, "[your work] testifies to the preeminent maturity you have acquired during past years and which remains unequalled" (Grubrich-Simitis, 1986, p. 271). In the "Confusion of tongues" paper, Ferenczi summarized all his work of the past several years with traumatized patients (which was fully explicated in the *Clinical Diary* that he had just written) and concluded: (1) that not everything was drive related and that early sexual trauma had severe consequences such as severe dissociation, denial, and identification with the aggressor.

GG 6

2) that sexual abuse does happen; (3) that the seducer convinces the victim that what is being given in the relationship is affection, love, tenderness and support, whereas the seducer is actually aggressing against the victim, intruding their needs into the experience of their partner which then allows for full domination, control and power over the victim; and (4) that the relationship with the aggressor was crucial. Therefore, if something awful has happened the aggressive person's denying it can be the real trauma (and by implication, the analyst's denying the trauma can also be re-traumatizing). Thus, the real confusion of tongues is what leads the victim to a deep loss of self and reality. Freud apparently felt Ferenczi was going back to his original seduction hypothesis and throwing out intrapsychic conflict and denying the worth of so many of his ideas that had developed from 1923 on in terms of defense analysis and the structural theory; whereas Ferenczi felt he was talking about what he had discovered with his very traumatized patients in the *Clinical Diary* (and what he had discovered about himself), where he understood that these patients had to reexperience their trauma in a safe environment. As many have felt, there was a true confusion of tongues between these two men. Since Ferenczi was very sick with pernicious anemia and using all of his energy to care for his deeply disturbed patients, Freud seemed to take this as his withdrawing and showing hostility towards him. Both of them were primed to misinterpret the other. Freud felt that all his work was being attacked, and Ferenczi felt

that his deeply-felt work was being dismissed as nonsense or at best as going back to an old theory. Freud actually tried to prevent Ferenczi from presenting his paper at the Congress that year (which was unheard of in psychoanalytic circles) and was so distressed that he told Jones that Ferenczi was not of sound mind. These words would be used many years later to demonize Ferenczi. I believe that Freud may have felt attacked on a much more personal level since his reaction was so unusually intense. Since the main point in Ferenczi's paper had to do with the authority's using and misusing the child and then denying it, I wonder if Freud may have felt that Ferenczi was saying that Freud was one of those analysts that retraumatizes their patients since he had denied Ferenczi the care he needed, and in his mutual analysis Ferenczi had discovered his own sexual abuse. If you read the *Clinical Diary* there is a sense that Ferenczi felt that Freud was destroying him by his lack of understanding and had a desperate need for his help.

GG 7

Freud clearly felt attacked and lashed out. Nevertheless, in the obituary Freud gave upon Ferenczi's death, Freud said that Ferenczi was the analyst to all analysts (Freud, 1933) and in *Analysis Terminable and Interminable* (one of Freud's last technique papers) he was still trying to justify why he didn't help Ferenczi more (Freud, 1937). In his explanation he states that one can't analyze a conflict that isn't present in the treatment, referring to Ferenczi's unconscious hostility towards him.

After Ferenczi died in 1933, many of Ferenczi's analysands went to England before and after the war. Balint wanted to publish Ferenczi's work and the correspondence, but it was tabled by Anna Freud who thought there were too many sensitive things to have it published. The "Confusion of Tongues between the Adults and the Child" paper was published in 1933 in the *International Zeitschrift für Psychoanalyse*, in German, and in English in 1949 in the *IJP* (not as early as had been promised to Ferenczi by Jones, the editor of the *International Journal of Psychoanalysis*) but not the *Diary* or the correspondence, which Balint insisted had to be published together. What made matters worse was that Jones (an ex-patient of Ferenczi) wrote in his biography of Freud (Jones, 1957) that all the papers that were written by Ferenczi at the end of his life were by a man who was suffering a psychosis induced by his illness.

GG 8

While many people including Balint, Ferenczi's wife, Gisella, her daughters, and especially Erich Fromm, who interviewed many people who had been with Ferenczi at the time of his death (Bonomi, 1998), verified that none of this was true, the fact that Anna Freud stood by Jones kept this myth alive. This was particularly ironic since Anna Freud, a lay analyst, was one of the people Ferenczi fought for (since he was a big proponent of lay analysis). Jones, who had never been a favorite son to Freud (and was actually distrusted by Freud), clearly revenged himself on his ex-analyst. As Judith Dupont (1988, p. 250) said in the introduction to the *Clinical Diary*,

"It is astonishing to realize how the entire psychoanalytic community, with few exceptions, readily accepted Jones declaration that Ferenczi was insane during the last three years of his life. Jones supported his assertion on the basis of statements of a witness of Ferenczi's last days, a witness whose name Jones refused to reveal and who to this day, has never been found. Yet most known witnesses deny categorically this so-called madness of Ferenczi. This can be seen as a symptom, a sign of resistance by the psychoanalytic world to something Ferenczi would have wanted to introduce to psychoanalysis."

It was interesting in my exploration of the problem of lay analysis in the U.S. that I found notes from the meetings of the New York Psychoanalytic Society on December 18, 1963, when Sandor Lorand (who had been an analysand of

Ferenczi's in 1923–24) presented parts of the book he was writing on pioneers in psychoanalysis in order to correct distortions and inaccuracies from the Jones biography (which had come out a few years earlier). He "reiterated that from 1908, when Ferenczi met Freud for the first time, Sándor Ferenczi played a heroic part, second only to Freud, in building psychoanalysis into a branch of science". Turning to his terminal illness, Dr. Lorand felt there was not a shred of evidence to indicate that Ferenczi ever suffered from personality impairment or mental illness, with the exception of the last weeks of his life, when his spinal cord and perhaps his brain were attacked in the terminal phase of pernicious anemia. In conclusion, Dr. Lorand remarked that "among the contributors to psychoanalysis, there is no one with the exception of Freud himself who contributed so many valuable and original ideas, no one who did as much as Ferenczi to develop psychoanalysis and bring it to the status it enjoys today." Dr. Ludwig Eidelberg then stood up and said that Ferenczi was the most charming man he had ever met and the best lecturer (Ferenczi had been in New York in 1926–1927). He recalled the advice of Nietzsche that great men should disguise their greatness to avoid the envy of those who work hard and produce little (Lorand, 1964, p. 469). Was he referring to Jones? I never heard anyone comment on these remarks that were made at New York Psychoanalytic Institute in 1963, and I'm sure people are surprised to learn about this given all the institutional silence that followed.

This brings me to the main point of this paper, which is to question why the contemporary Freudians in the 80s didn't rejoice when the *Clinical Diary* and the correspondence finally came out. Other groups quickly claimed Ferenczi as their own. It is a tragic story to see how his ideas were concealed for so long by the analytic community in Europe and more so in the US. Adrienne Harris and Lew Aaron made a major contribution by publishing their 1993 book on the legacy of Sándor Ferenczi, which included many of the people that had helped to preserve Ferenczi's work, especially Judith Dupont (Aron & Harris, 1993).

I will try to show that we don't have to go back to 1933, and the strong reaction Freud had to the "Confusion of tongues" paper to see psychoanalytic politics at work. During the 80s and 90s, when the Ferenczi papers were finally published, Freudian thinking was already changing a great deal, as evidenced by papers by Stone (1961) and Jacobs (1986). And the reaction to Ferenczi could have easily been very welcoming. Instead, the relational movement, which basically started with Greenberg and Mitchell's 1983 book *Object Relations in Psychoanalytic Theory* and Stephen Mitchells 1988 book *Relational Concepts in Psychoanalysis,* quickly acknowledged Ferenczi's contributions and ran with them (even if they did exaggerate his emphasis on mutuality and used it to attack the classical Freudian model). I maintain that for some Freudians (whom Steve Ellman has called "the self and object" Freudians in *The Modern Freudians* and then later named the Contemporary Freudians) their position about the role of the analyst was already changing but the battlegrounds were drawn up between the role of the analyst and the role of interpretation and intrapsychic conflict.

My growing-up years in psychoanalytic training were definitely a study in being in or out. I will try to show that certain people who were somewhat outside the Freudian system (like Winnicott) were forgiven many transgressions because the Freudians didn't target him as a traitor. Nor did he threaten their power structure within the psychoanalytic situation or in their institutes. His personality wasn't an object of scrutiny. I am not trying to demonize Winnicott but just trying to show how one overlooks certain things if they don't threaten the status quo. It is disturbing and frightening that one can be trained to try and know the truth and yet never question the depths of one's distortions about the other. In fact, when the relational movement began in the 1980s and Ferenczi's *Clinical Dairy* came out (the same year as Mitchell's book), followed by the 4 volumes of the correspondence starting in

1993 and ending in 2000, psychoanalysis was in a state of flux. Ferenczi's papers were allowed to be published after Anna Freud's death on October 9, 1982, and the first Ferenczi conference was in 1991. The Ferenczi Center was started at the New School in 2008 (where Ferenczi had taught during the six months he was in the U.S.).

(GG9)

1988 was also the time when a Federal anti-trust class action lawsuit was decided in favor of the four psychologist plaintiffs who had sued the American Psychoanalytic Association, the International Psychoanalytical Association, and two institutes affiliated with these associations for restraint of trade. It was in 1991 that the APsaA finally modified its by-laws to eliminate the waiver process for full clinical psychoanalytic training for doctoral level psychologists and social workers. It was an amazing time in psychoanalysis. What you may not know is that Ferenczi tried to start a group of lay analysts when he was here in 1927, much to the dismay of the analysts at the New York Psychoanalytic Institute, and it was disbanded in 1929. Their objection to his passionate stand on lay analysis was the reason he didn't stay in the U.S. Yet many of them went to him for treatment when he was here (Dupont, 2000).

What could have been so disturbing to the Freudians about Ferenczi's ideas? I will give a little summary of the papers that were coming out in the 70s and 80s in the Freudian literature for you to have some feeling for what the background was when the Ferenczi papers surfaced. The most important part of Ferenczi's ideas, besides his extraordinary work on trauma and the identification with the aggressor, had to do with the therapeutic relationship, the early development of the self and how to make a safe environment, especially for patients who had early maternal deprivation, and his focus on process analysis. I will get to more of his contributions later but for the Freudians long before 1988, we already had Leo Stone's 1961 book *The Psychoanalytic Situation*, which had an enormous impact on my thinking. It is noteworthy that I read that book several times because of my interest in the classical Freudian view of the blank screen, which led to my paper on anonymity (C. Ellman, 2011). I never noticed until I read Ferenczi that Stone was fascinated with all the techniques that Ferenczi had used and spent a great deal of that book in dialogue with some of Ferenczi's ideas. In 1968, we had Racker's book *Transference and Countertransference* (Racker, 1968) followed by Joseph Sandler's very important paper on role responsiveness (Sandler, 1976). In 1981, we had McLaughlin's paper "Transference, psychic reality and countertransference," followed by his 1991 paper "Clinical and theoretical aspects of enactment" (McLaughlin, 1981, 1991). We had Grunes's 1984 paper "The therapeutic object relationship" and then Ted Jacobs's important 1986 paper "On countertransference enactments," followed by his 1991 book *The Use of the Self.* In 1991, Judith Chused wrote "The evocative power of enactments" (Chused, 1991). All of these papers ushered in the understanding of the importance of the role of the analyst in the process of working through unconscious fantasies that can't be worked through by interpretation alone and how important the analyst's role was in the process.

At the same time that these important ideas were coming out, the therapeutic relationship, the emphasis on early development, and the treatment of narcissistic pathology were being discussed in Kohut's papers in 1968 and 1971 on the treatment of the narcissistic personality (Kohut, 1968, 1971) and of course in Sheldon Bach's extraordinary work starting in 1985 with *Narcissistic States and the Therapeutic Process* (Bach, 1985). Loewald's papers had already come out starting in the 60s and culminating in 1980 with his collected papers (Loewald, 1980), which strongly emphasized the developmental model in treatment and the role of the analyst, who was no longer a blank screen. Equally important was the 1975 publication of *The Psychological Birth of the Human Infant* by Mahler, Pine and Bergmann (Mahler,

Pine, Bergmann, 1975). Our thoughts were shifting more and more to early deficits and trauma.

You can see from the papers I am citing that already in the 70s and 80s before the Freud-Ferenczi letters came out and the *Clinical Diary*, for some Freudians the technique was already changing. When relational psychoanalysis came about, not only were many Freudians writing about enactment (e.g., Jacobs, 1986; Sandler, 1976) but some like Mahler (1975) were writing about the importance of the early mother-child relationship.

So why didn't some Freudians also claim Ferenczi as a mentor the way the relational group did? And why did the relational group attack the Freudian model at the time as if it wasn't changing at all? Why did we in 1989 rush to read Shengold's *Soul Murder* (Shengold, 1989) and not Ferenczi's *Clinical Diary*, which had appeared the year before, even though both publications were about severe trauma? Plus, in our work weren't we already talking about the importance of the relationship, the early holding that needed to occur with disturbed patients, the need for role responsiveness? Didn't I say in my introduction to *The Modern Freudians* in 1998 that the role of the analyst was now an important part of technique? We were happy to let the other groups claim this brilliant clinician and cling to mistaken ideas (that few of us knew were just rumors and distortions) of what he really said and did with patients and of why Freud and he had parted ways. I will argue that psychoanalytic politics has always looked for scapegoats in order to make their group more cohesive and that we are constantly reinventing ourselves while we try and demonize the other, often to find that some of their points (including the relational challenge) were important and needed to be integrated into our work.

Something was also threatening about Ferenczi's ideas. Partly, they were threatening because you had to be very present in the room with the patient, the way Shelly Bach taught me to try and enter their world. Ferenczi searched for a long time (trying many different techniques) to try and work with difficult patients. He realized he had to pay attention to some things that went beyond words (such as projective identifications, enactments, the need for an early holding environment). He was very sensitive to anything about the analyst's role that might recreate the trauma of childhood by treating everything as intrapsychic, when someone had been abused. In reading his work, I don't think he was a self-psychologist or a relational analyst or a Kleinian or a Contemporary Freudian (although he always thought there was a strong need to get to unconscious fantasy when the patient was capable of that). When I think about why he was demonized for so long, I don't think it was only his so-called disloyalty to Freud, but I think his model of treatment was a threat in and of itself. Teaching students to listen without dogma is very difficult. The schools that were created after the war were very dominated by theory (which is exactly what Ferenczi disliked). Besides, the trauma of Ferenczi's death, the trauma of Freud's death in 1939, and the dissolution of psychoanalysis as it was known before the war, left everyone looking for someone to identify with and to try and keep psychoanalysis alive. Many theories (and schools) developed that were very far from looking at the clinical data. It took more than 30 years for Kleinians to start realizing that patients with narcissistic defenses cannot hear deep interpretations, for Freudians to incorporate not only unconscious fantasy but the important role of the early environment and the analyst as more than a blank screen, for relational therapists to start realizing that everything wasn't about the relationship but that patients also came with unconscious conflicts, etc. Not only did Ferenczi feel that one had to look at process, and look at one's own deep reactions to patients, he was determined to try and cure people and if they weren't getting better, he was willing to try something else. He was a clinician who had a complex way of listening and that is why the most difficult cases were sent to him. Martin Bergmann, one of the few analysts in America who were writing about Ferenczi, said in a 1996 paper, "The tragic encounter between Freud and Ferenczi," "Ferenczi...offered his analysands unconditional understanding and a right to find their own path to cure. In my view, it is hard enough to be a creative analyst on Freud's model; it is next to impossible to live up to Ferenczi's." (Bergmann, 1996, p. 154)

I maintain that most theories of technique simplify what the analyst should do (be a blank screen, always interpret the aggression, reflect empathic failures, only interpret the transference, etc.). For Ferenczi, establishing trust (as S. Ellman, 2007 emphasizes) was crucial across techniques. He knew establishing trust with patients with early deprivation was very difficult. Freud actually knew he couldn't be that type of clinician (Haynal, 1993), and my guess is that many of Ferenczi's colleagues knew that they couldn't either.

I don't think in the 80s many Freudians (especially the more classically trained) were embracing their own genius clinicians such as Stone and Kohut and Bach. Because of the threat of the relational movement, they had to define themselves as analysts that (1) do not indulge their patients, (2) are much stricter and disciplined with their patients, (3) are much better analyzed than their colleagues in other groups, and (4) believe in the unconscious and transference which made them the true heirs of Freud. While the relational group was constantly focusing on the classical Freudian position, which did have its vulnerabilities, I think many Freudians who were paying attention to object relations theory still had an idealization of classical technique and had their own identity crisis about who they were and who they were becoming. The paper I wrote in 2011 on anonymity (C. Ellman, 2011) had many positions that Stone and Bach proposed, but people still asked me if I was relational? There seemed to be a threat to one's identity to focus on the relationship and not just on intrapsychic conflict.

It has been fascinating to me to contrast the way many Freudians accepted Winnicott (who in many ways was more in a direct line to Ferenczi in his desire to cure). It's not that the Freudians at the New York Psychoanalytic Institute treated Winnicott kindly in 1968 when he presented his paper "The use of an object" and was treated with such scorn (Baudry, 2009), but for the rest of us trained with a somewhat more object relational background, we were intrigued by Winnicott's ideas, but we overlooked the following facts. Winnicott's role with Masud Kahn is fairly well known now in terms of how he used him to edit his papers, didn't really analyze the narcissistic transference, and didn't help with his deep destructiveness (Hopkins, 2006). But more than anything, many of the ways that Winnicott worked with patients such as Margaret Little are similar to Ferenczi's work in the *Clinical Diary,* where he encouraged regression. As Margaret Little says in her book about her analysis with Winnicott:

> Literally through many long hours he held my two hands clasped between his almost like an umbilical cord, while I lay often hidden beneath the blanket, silent, inert, withdrawn, in panic, rage or tears, asleep and sometimes dreaming. Sometimes, he would become drowsy, fall asleep and wake with a jerk, to which I would react with anger, terrified and feeling as if I had been hit (Little, 1991, p. 44).

He also adapted himself to her rhythm, extending sessions to ninety minutes when he became aware that nothing happened for the first portion of the session. Patients often slept in the other room until they could continue the work. Many of the things we see Ferenczi doing for his regressed patients were actually very much followed by Winnicott. Winnicott, however, would reveal many things to patients about his health and his depression. What is interesting reading some accounts of Winnicott's work (and many of his patients were extremely attached to him and his caring ways) is that there is no indication that Winnicott analyzed himself in the same way Ferenczi did. Winnicott had many failed treatments, but we don't read about the constant corrections that Ferenczi kept making. Ferenczi worried all the time whether he was doing the right thing and left us a diary which Winnicott didn't (as far as I know). The other difference, as far as I can tell, is that we had access to all of Winnicott's writings and could think about his ideas and therefore hardly dwelt on his personal faults. Whereas Ferenczi's writings were hidden and we were flooded with false rumors about him as a person. The "Confusion of tongues" paper came out in 1949. Winnicott clearly picked up where Ferenczi left off. But we do not know what he knew of Ferenczi's ideas from Balint, Rickman or Klein who were Ferenczi's patients, since Winnicott rarely referenced his sources. I do believe however that if one studies the history of ideas many things come together at the same time making it hard to pinpoint the exact source.

GG 10

Some of the ideas in Ferenczi's papers include:

1. He radically challenged the relatively safe attitude of the analyst as a blank screen, and he saw analysis as an emotionally taxing, involving enterprise. He felt analysts often choose an intellectualized approach, not always according to the needs of the therapy, but often according to their own needs.

2. He drew attention to the communicative value of dreams, postures, and all movements in the analytic space in addition to verbal content.

3. He drew attention to the countertransference problems in training analyses and even though he helped to start the IPA, he worried that institutes could rigidly serve the analyst's own needs and not the patients.

4. He stressed the central role of intuition, empathy, and trust, especially with the most difficult cases and wanted to add techniques which would allow the treatment of cases until then unreachable by psychoanalysis.

5. He thought one must think in terms of analytic process and a new way of listening to material where everything happening in the room was important.

6. He recognized the importance of mourning and the effects of a maternal object that wasn't good enough so that one had to take into consideration problems of abandonment when one saw narcissistic withdrawal in patients.

7. He started to understand the analyst's contribution to creating a working environment to help the patient symbolize, anticipating some of Bion's thoughts.

8. Most of all, his work on trauma is exemplary; not only did he highlight the power of witnessing and accepting the patient's story but the identification with the aggressor and loss of self that Jay Frankel has highlighted so beautifully in his articles which should be required reading.

9. If one reads the *Clinical Diary*, one realizes that Ferenczi predated all the analysts that felt that early attachment led to the foundation of a sense of self and a capacity for trust. Without a good holding environment, Ferenczi felt, one couldn't sustain a sense of agency, and one was prone more to falseness and submission. He didn't use the term false self, and he was more interested in the fragmented self, but his emphasis on how the self develops through containment and holding anticipates Winnicott.

10. He also felt that when a treatment reached an impasse, he insisted on the analyst searching himself for negative countertransference and, more than anything, on his being honest. Dupont says that he tried to give his wounded, hypersensitive patients with fragmented selves the means to locate their analyst, to identify with him, and to be able to feel to what extent they could count on him.

Aron and Harris said in 2010, "The rediscovery of Ferenczi has been the recognition of an appalling familiar and institutional tragedy, ridden with Oedipal disappointment and struggles and fratricidal battles. It is to unearth a buried trauma. The presentation and publication of Ferenczi's 'Confusion of tongues' paper on the powerful traumatizing effect of incest and families' collusive silence must rank among the oldest and most tragic moments in the history of psychoanalysis" (Aron and Harris, 2010). I would add that the Contemporary Freudians' not embracing Ferenczi as their forefather/mother in terms of the contemporary understanding of the importance of the therapeutic relationship to enable trust and his deep understanding of early developmental ruptures is just as sad, since many people writing at that time (Loewald, Sandler, Bach, Stone) were telling us the very same thing. Analysis cures by a certain type of love that means an engagement and caring for the patient and flexibility with more disturbed patients. It is these elements that help the patient get to their deeper unconscious conflicts. Sheldon Bach would also pick up this theme of love in the analytic situation later on in his work (Bach, 2006).

Apparently Ferenczi was a loveable person, rich in vitality and zest for living. Many (even in New York) considered him the warmest, most human, most sensitive of the early psychoanalytic group. But more than anything he cared so deeply about his patients, and that quality is what drew me to him. After I read Ferenczi I understood identification with the aggressor in a whole new way. His ability to take you into the experience of a needy dependent child/person who is being abused and how that person can slowly surrender their self to the other is something that I have used over and over in my work with patients that have suffered such devastation. His ability to describe their pain is unlike any other writer since he writes from the inside not as an observer. Eve Ensler's (2019) *The Apology* is the only thing that I have read that comes as close to living it with the person.

Finding an answer to the most perfect technique is an ongoing process. Perfect for whom and which therapist. I remember when I wrote my anonymity paper, I asked supervisees whether they really knew that a blank screen led to the most associations for all patients? I gave many examples and asked them never to accept something as dogma unless it was clear it was based on what they observed and was clearly best for that particular patient. When I read Stone and I worked with Shelly Bach, I knew they were thinking about what made patients safe when they talked about technique. When I read Ferenczi, I knew most of all he wanted to help his patients even if he went to extremes with his most disturbed patients. He experimented, he changed his methods when they didn't work, and he knew when he reached blind spots. He knew he needed more analysis because he deeply appreciated the depths of the unconscious, but Freud his analyst wasn't there for him.

I am going to end with a passage from the "Confusion of tongues" paper for you to hear Ferenczi's voice in describing the reaction to abuse:

"One would expect the first impulse [to abuse] to be that of rejection, hatred, disgust and energetic refusal. 'No, no, I do not want it, it is much too violent for me, it hurts, leave me alone', this or something similar would be the immediate reaction if it would not be paralyzed by enormous anxiety. These children feel physically and morally helpless, their personalities are not sufficiently consolidated in order to be able to protest, even if only in thought, for the overpowering force and authority of the adult makes them dumb and can rob them of their senses. *The same anxiety, however, if it reaches a certain maximum, compels them to subordinate themselves like automata to the will of the aggressor, to divine each one of his desires and to gratify these; completely oblivious of themselves they identify themselves with the aggressor.* [...] In any case, the attack as a rigid external reality ceases to exist and in the traumatic trance the child succeeds in maintaining the previous situation of tenderness.

147

The most important change, produced in the mind of a child by the anxiety-fear-ridden identification with the adult partner, is *the introjection of the guilt feelings of the adult* which makes hitherto harmless play appear as a punishable offense.

When the child recovers from such an attack, he feels enormously confused, in fact, split—innocent and culpable at the same time—and his confidence in the testimony of his own senses is broken" (Ferenczi, 1949, p. 227) (italics in the original).

Psychoanalysis is an amazing field—especially the understanding of the unconscious and the psychoanalytic situation that Freud invented—but just like any other human endeavor, it has its flaws. What happened with Ferenczi not only showed how human we are but how envy, belonging, scapegoating, and the will to power are such basic human drives that even the best of us is privy to such primitive needs to find pleasure in exclusion. When I worked with Sheldon Bach I knew I was finding my way back to what was lost when Ferenczi's words and spirit were banned.

References

Aron, L., & Harris, A. (1993) (Eds). *The Legacy of Sándor Ferenczi*. Hillsdale, NJ: The Analytic Press.

—— & —— (2010). A New (2010) Introduction to Aron and Harris (1993) *Sándor Ferenczi: Discovery and Rediscovery*. An introduction to *The Legacy of Sándor Ferenczi. Psychoanalytic Perspectives*, 7(1), 1-4.

Bach, S. (1985). *Narcissistic states and the therapeutic process*. Northvale, NJ: Jason Aronson.

—— (2006). *Getting From Here to There: Analytic Love, Analytic Process*. New York: Routledge.

———— (2016). *Chimeras and Other Writings: Selected Papers of Sheldon Bach*. New York: IPBooks.

Balint, M. (1968). *The basic fault: Therapeutic aspects of regression*. Evanston, IL: Northwestern University Press.

Baudry, F. (2009). Winnicott's 1968 visit to the New York Psychoanalytic Society and Institute: a contextual view. *Psychoanalytic Quarterly,* 78(4),1059–1090.

Bergmann, M.S. (1996). The tragic encounter between Freud and Ferenczi. In *Ferenczi's turn in psychoanalysis*. P. Rudnytsky, A. Bokay, & P. Giampieri-Deutsch (Eds.) New York: New York University Press.

Bion, W.R. (1959) Attacks on Linking. *International Journal of Psychoanalysis.* 40:308–315.

Bonomi, C. (1998). Jones's allegation of Ferenczi's mental deterioration: a reassessment. *International Forum of Psychoanalysis*, 7(4):201–206.

Britton, R. (1989). The missing link: parental sexuality in the Oedipus complex. In R. Britton, M. Feldman, E. O'Shaughnessy, & J. Steiner (Eds.) *The Oedipus complex today: Clinical implications*. London, UK: Karnac Books.

Chused, J.F. (1991). The evocative power of enactments. *Journal of the American Psychoanalytic Association,* 39:615–639.

Druck, A.B., Ellman, C.S., Freedman, N., & Thaler, A. (2011) (Eds.). *A new Freudian Synthesis: Clinical process in the next generation*. London, UK: Karnac Books.

Ellman, C.S. (2011). Anonymity: blank screen or black hole. In: A. B. Druck, C.S. Ellman, N. Freedman, and A. Thaler, (Eds.) *A new Freudian synthesis: clinical process in the next generation*. London, UK: Karnac Books.

———— Grand, S., Silvan, M., & Ellman, S.J. (1998) (Eds.). *The Modern Freudians: Contemporary Psychoanalytic Technique.* Northvale, N.J: Jason Aronson.

Ellman, S.J. (1998). The unique contribution of the contemporary Freudian position. In C.S. Ellman, S. Grand, M. Silvan, & S.J. Ellman, eds. (1998). *The modern Freudians: contemporary psychoanalytic technique.* Northvale, NJ: Jason Aronson.

———— (2007). Analytic trust and transference: love, healing ruptures and facilitating repairs. *Psychoanalytic Inquiry:* 27:246–263.

Ensler, E. (2019). *The Apology.* London, UK: Bloomsbury Publishing.

Faimberg, H. (2005). *The Telescoping of Generations.* London, UK: Routledge.

Ferenczi, S., & Rank, O. (1925). *The development of psychoanalysis.* New York and Washington: Nervous and Mental Diseases Publishing Co.

Frankel, J. (2002). Exploring Ferenczi's concept of identification with the aggressor: its role in trauma, everyday life, and the therapeutic relationship. *Psychoanalytic Dialogues,* 12:101–139.

Freud, S. (1923). Two encyclopedia articles. *Standard Edition,* 18:253, quoted in C.S. Ellman, S. Grand, M. Silvan, & S. J. Ellman. (1998). *The modern Freudians: contemporary psychoanalytic technique.* Northvale, NJ: Jason Aronson.

———— (1933). Sándor Ferenczi. *Standard Edition,* 22:227–229.

———— (1937). Analysis terminable and interminable. *Standard Edition,* 23:216–253.

Greenberg, J. R., & Mitchell, S. A. (1983). *Object Relations in Psychoanalytic Theory*. Cambridge, MA: Harvard University Press.

Greenson, R. R. (1965). The working alliance and the transference neurosis. *Psychoanalytic Quarterly*, 34:155–181.

Grossmark, R. (2018). The unobtrusive relational group analyst and the work of the narrative. *Psychoanalytic Inquiry*, 38 246–255.

Grubrich-Simitis, I. (1986). Six letters of Sigmund Freud and Sándor Ferenczi on the interrelationship of psychoanalytic theory and technique. Letter Freud to Ferenczi, January 4, 1928. *International Review of Psychoanalysis*, 13:259–277.

Grunes, M. (1984). The therapeutic object relationship. *Psychoanalytic Review*, 17: 123–144.

Haynal, A. E. (1989). *The technique at issue: Controversies in Psychoanalytic Method: From Freud and Ferenczi to Michael Balint*. New York: New York University Press.

Haynal, A. (1992). Introduction. In *The correspondence of Sigmund Freud and Sándor Ferenczi Volume 1. 1908–1914*. E. Brabant, E. Falzeder & P. Giampieri-Deutsch (Eds.), P. T. Hoffer (Trans.). With an Introduction by and under the supervision of A. Haynal. Cambridge, Mass. &London, England: The Belknap Press of Harvard University Press. pp. xvii–xxxv.

Hopkins, L. (2006). *False self: The life of Masud Kahn*. London, UK: Other Press.

Jacobs, T.J. (1986). Countertransference enactments. *Journal of the American Psychoanalytic Association*, 34:289–307.

———(1991). *The Use of the Self*. Madison, CT: International Universities Press.

Jones, E. (1957). *Sigmund Freud: Life and Work*. Vol. 3. London, UK: Hogarth Press.

Kohut, H. (1968). The psychoanalytic treatment of narcissistic personality disorders—outline of a systematic approach. *Psychoanalytic Study of the Child*, 23:86–113.

———— (1971). *The analysis of the self: A systematic approach to the treatment of narcissistic personality disorders*. New York: International Universities Press.

———— (1972). Thoughts on narcissism and narcissistic rage. *Psychoanalytic Study of the Child, 27:* 360–400.

Little, M. (1991). *Psychotic anxieties and containment: A personal record of an analysis with Winnicott*. Northvale, NJ: Jason Aronson.

Loewald, H.W. (1960). On the therapeutic action of psychoanalysis. *International Journal of Psychoanalysis*, 41:16–33.

———— (1980). *Papers on Psychoanalysis*. New Haven: Yale University Press.

Lorand, S. (1964). Meetings of the Psychoanalytic Association of New York. December 16, 1963. *Psychoanalytic Quarterly*, 33,:68–469.

Lugrin, Y. (2021). *Ferenczi on Freud's Couch: A Finished Analysis?* New York: Routledge.

Mahler, M. S., Pine, F., & Bergman, A. (1975). *The psychological birth of the human infant: Symbiosis and individuation*. New York: Basic Books.

McLaughlin, J.T. (1981). Transference, Psychic Reality, and Countertransference. *Psychoanalytic Quarterly, 50:* 639–664.

———— (1991). Clinical and Theoretical Aspects of Enactment. *Journal of the American Psychoanalytic Association*, 39: 95–614.

Mitchell, S. A. (1988). *Relational concepts in psychoanalysis: An integration.* Cambridge, MA: Harvard University Press.

Rachman, A. W. (2017). Elizabeth Severn: The "evil genius" of psychoanalysis. London, UK: Routledge.

Racker, H. (1968). *Transference and Countertransference.* London: Routledge.

Sandler, J. (1976). Countertransference and Role-Responsiveness. *International Review of Psychoanalysis,* 3:43–47.

Shengold, L. (1989). *Soul murder: the effects of childhood abuse and deprivation.* New York, NY: Fawcett Columbine.

Stone, L. (1961). *The Psychoanalytic situation: an examination of its development and essential nature.* New York, NY: International Universities Press.

Giselle Galdi Comments

GG1

Thank you for including me in the process of commenting on Dr. Carolyn Ellman's excellent scholarly paper. The topic of her paper is close to my heart, as a Hungarian-American psychoanalyst. I have been involved in the Ferenczi renaissance for many years, and I also admire Sheldon Bach's work and writings. His work often reminds me of the Ferenczian spirit.

A few brief points.

Please note: her name was Gizella Ferenczi, with a "z" not Gisella. Gisela—with one "l" is the German version. However, Ferenczi's wife never signed anything the German way. Just like Ferenczi was always Sándor, the Hungarian name, not Alexander, the German version. In his German language letters, Freud always addressed Ferenczi's wife as **Frau Gizella.**

It is a bit reductionistic to characterize this an "affair", i.e., emphasizing the sexual aspects, given the complex intruding and gossiping by both Freud and Ferenczi about the treatment of Elma. Roazen, 1998, called it "psychoanalytically inspired meddling in Elma's life."

I would recommend the 3 volume Freud & Ferenczi correspondence (Freud & Ferenczi 1908–1914, 1914–1919, 1920–1933) as a main source for this subject.

GG 2

Vilma Kovács should be added to the list. Mahler was not analyzed by Ferenczi. He introduced psychoanalysis to her when as a very young person she was a frequent visitor at the Kovács residence, and the Ferenczi circle and was greatly influenced by him. Mahler's analysts were August Aichhorn, Helene Deutsch, and Willi Hoffer. On Spitz—Ferenczi was one of his teachers in Budapest, but Spitz's analyst was Freud. To the best of my knowledge, Otto Rank was neither analyzed by Ferenczi nor Freud. He had a very close, intimate personal relationship with Freud until their fallout. Also, Rank collaborated with Ferenczi in the 1920s, but he was not analyzed by anyone as far as I know. Theresa Benedek should be added to the list of Ferenczi's analysands too.

GG 3

The word, Totschweigen, had been used when Menaker lived in Vienna. I would characterize Rachman's reference to her as anecdotal. Actually, the idea of Totschweigen goes back to the very early days of the psychoanalytic world. Freud's disapproval of anyone who went their own way, or was not sufficiently loyal to him, led to exclusion of the "disloyal" person, followed by systematic silence, see Jung, Adler, Rank, Tausk, etc. And one of the glaring examples of Totschweigen was Ferenczi because of his last years of disagreements with Freud's perspectives about clinical work, trauma and the role of sexual drives in the nature of the UCS mind (See Ferenczi's 1915 "Dialogue of the Unconsciouses", a relational concept of the UCS). After Freud's death, the Holocaust and major displacements of European psychoanalysts, his loyal followers tightly held onto every word of Freud, and carried on with Ferenczi's dismissal, exclusion. For example, Ferenczi's role in the history of psychoanalysis was so fully repressed that "This presidency of the International Psychanalytical

Association has been all but forgotten, and it was only in 1996 that the former President of the IPA, Horacio Etchegoyen, noticed a glaring omission in the portrait gallery of Presidents in Broomhills—Sándor Ferenczi'"(Falzeder & Dupont, 2000; Bonomi, 1999, p. 507).

Another example, "psychoanalysts seemed to have "discovered" countertransference in the late 1940s and early '50s. It is still a widely accepted notion that it was Racker who in 1952 first systematically widened Freud's original view of countertransference—an obstruction to the work, stemming from the analysts' resistances and unresolved conflicts—an idea that was sustained by the five-decades-long **"Totschweigen"** (death by silence) of Ferenczi. In fact, Ferenczi was the first who explored the analyst's deep involvement with the analytic process in connection with the so-called "difficult patient." (Galdi, 1998, p. 3).

Axel Hoffer (1991, p. 466) wrote:

> "An admittedly oversimplified metaphor provides a frame to begin our inquiry: if Sigmund Freud was the father of psychoanalysis, Sándor Ferenczi was the mother. Psychoanalysis lost its mother through Ferenczi's untimely death of pernicious anemia in 1933 at a time when each man was profoundly upset and disillusioned with the other. Psychoanalysis thus became a one-parent child. Ferenczi's work on the early dyadic mother-child relationship and its reliving in the analytic situation came to a premature end."

GG 4

It was called the "kissing technique" letter, in Freud's words (Freud & Ferenczi, 1920–1933, Freud's letter to Ferenczi, December 13, 1931; also described by Ferenczi in the *Clinical Diary*, the entry on January 7, 1932, titled, *Insensitivity of the Analyst*. Ferenczi writes: "See the case of Dm. [Ferenczi's code for Clara Thompson], a lady who, 'complying' with my passivity, had allowed herself to take more and more liberties, and occasionally even kissed me. Since this behavior met with no resistance, since it was treated as something permissible in analysis and at most commented on theoretically: [Connected to Ferenczi's technical experiments with analytic abstinence, his "principle of relaxation", 1930], she remarked quite casually in the company of other patients, who were undergoing analysis elsewhere: 'I am allowed to kiss Papa Ferenczi, as often as I like.' I first reacted to the unpleasantness that ensued with the complete impassivity with which I was conducting this analysis. It was only through the insight and admission that my passivity had been unnatural that she was brought back to real life. It became evident … that as a child, Dm. had been grossly abused sexually by her father, obviously because of the father's bad conscience and social anxiety, he reviled her. The daughter had to take revenge on her father indirectly, by failing in her own life" (Ferenczi, 1932, pp. 2–3).

GG 5

The analysis of Elma with Ferenczi, at the suggestion of her mother, Gizella, started in July 1911, and went well for a few months. Then one of Elma's admirers killed himself, and Ferenczi wrote to Freud: "It is very questionable how the matter will go now." (See Ferenczi to Freud, October 18, 1911. Letter # 244, pp. 303–304). Elma became depressed and her transference toward Ferenczi took another turn (Freud & Ferenczi, 1908–1914, Letter # 252, p. 312). Ferenczi wrote: "Elma became especially dangerous to meet the moment when—after that young man's suicide—she badly needed someone to support her and *help* her in her need. I did that only too well; even though I held my tenderness in check with difficulty for the moment. But the path was cleared— and now, to all appearances, she has won my heart." Ferenczi also reminds Freud of his desire to have children which was not possible with the older Gizella. (Freud & Ferenczi, 1908–1914, December 3, 1911, Letter # 256, p. 318. Italicized by Ferenczi). In his research in London, in the 1960s, Paul Roazen asked Michael Balint about the alleged "intimacy between Ferenczi and Elma." Roazen writes: "Balint denied that there had been any sexual relationship but acknowledged that they had been very deeply in love" (Roazen, 1998, p. 275). Let's recall that Balint, the literary executor of Ferenczi's works, was very familiar with the correspondence between Freud and Ferenczi. Roazen also describes his reaction to the 1st Freud-Ferenczi volume of their correspondences (1908–1914), and the involvement of Freud and Ferenczi with Elma, Gizella, about Freud's treatment of Elma. Roazen comments on "Freud and Ferenczi's human impropriety of the psychoanalytically inspired meddling in Elma's life". etc. (Roazen, 1998, p. 282).

GG 6

Ferenczi's work (1932, 1933) preceded Anna Freud's 1936 work. We know that Anna attended Ferenczi's presentation in Wiesbaden, in September 1932, where Ferenczi talked about the identification with the aggressor. She was the observer for her father. Of course, when she published her 1936 book, her Father was still alive and under no circumstances could she refer to Ferenczi's work.

GG 7

Ferenczi writes in his *Diary* on October 2nd, 1932, after the Wiesbaden congress: "In my case the blood crisis arose when I realized that not only can I not rely on the protection of a 'higher power' but on the contrary I shall be trampled underfoot by this indifferent power as soon as I go my own way and not his. The insight this experience has helped me to attain is that I was brave (and productive) as long as I (unconsciously) relied for support on another power, that is, I had never really become 'grown up'.... And now, just as I must build new red corpuscles, must I (if I can) create a new basis for my personality, if I have to abandon as false and untrustworthy the one I have had up to now? Is the choice here one dying and 'rearranging myself'—and this at the age of fifty-nine?" (Ferenczi, 1932, p. 212).

GG8

The three-volume official biography of Freud, 1953–1957, by Ernest Jones, Ferenczi's former analysand, "overshadowed historical facts" regarding Ferenczi. Paul Roazen writes that in the present time (1998) when we start to recognize Ferenczi's true worth, it "may not be remembered how low Ferenczi's reputation had once sunk" (p. 271). In the mid-1960s, interviewing survivors who knew Ferenczi, Roazen had the chance to examine the correspondence between Michael Balint and Jones. He discovered how much Balint disagreed with Jones' characterization of Ferenczi's mental state. Also, in 1958, Erich Fromm protested about Jones' character assassination of Ferenczi, by orthodox classical analysts, strict followers of Freud and wedded to their certitude.

GG9

See account of Dupont, 2000, titled "Ferenczi's trip to the United Sates and the question of lay analysis," pp. xvii–xxix, on Ferenczi's the six-month visit at the New School, from September 1926 to March 1927. It is very worthwhile to read those pages by Dupont in the 3rd volume of the Freud-Ferenczi Correspondence. Dupont writes that the trip "foreshadowed the deepening rift between Freud and Ferenczi. **Freud felt abandoned by Ferenczi, he feared that Ferenczi would end up in America permanently**. He wrote above all of his failing health and his weariness. He seemed depressed and disillusioned."

GG10

Peter Rudnytsky (1991) describes that a lack of acknowledgment of sources was a common criticism directed at Winnicott. For example, Charles Rycroft, also complained about Winnicott's inability to cite the works of others. According to Rudnytsky's analysis in his 1991 book, *"The Psychoanalytic Vocation,"* Winnicott rarely acknowledged his sources or parallel ideas found in the works of other psychoanalysts. Rudnytsky describes how **Michael Balint,**

160

a fellow *Independent* analyst in the British Society, and a pupil and colleague of Ferenczi for many years, frequently called Winnicott's attention to the fact that he was using Ferenczi's ideas without referring to them. Winnicott admitted to his weakness of not acknowledging others who came before him and at a British Psychoanalytical Society meeting he explained that **he was not a librarian.**

References

Bach, S. (2000). Scientific Meeting of the Association for the Advancement of Psychoanalysis. A mind of one's own: Some observations on thinking disorders. Discussant: Giselle Galdi. *American Journal of Psychoanalysis, 60,* 393–396.

Bonomi, C. (1999). Flight into sanity. *International Journal of Psychoanalysis, 80,* 507–542. `

Dupont, J. (1988). Introduction. In S. Ferenczi (1932). *The Clinical Diary of Sándor Ferenczi,* J. Dupont (Ed.), M. Balint & N.Z. Jackson (Trans.). Cambridge, MA. & London: Harvard University Press. 1988. pp. xi–xxvii.

———— (1994). Freud's analysis of Ferenczi as revealed by their correspondence. *International Journal of Psycho-Analysis, 75,* 301–320.

———— (2000). Introduction. In Freud, S., & Ferenczi, S. (1920–1933). *The correspondence of Sigmund Freud and Sándor Ferenczi, Volume 3. 1920–1933.* E. Falzeder & E. Brabant (Eds.), with the collaboration of P. Giampieri-Deutsch under the supervision of A. Haynal. P. T. Hoffer (Trans.). With an Introduction by J. Dupont. Cambridge, MA & London: The Belknap Press of Harvard University Press. pp. xvii–xliv.

Falzeder, E., & Dupont, J. (2000). Sándor Ferenczi: The president of the International Psychoanalytical Association (1918–1920) and founder of the *International Journal of Psychoanalysis*. *International Journal of Psychoanalysis*, 81, 805–805.

Ferenczi, S. (1915). Psychogenic anomalies of voice production. In *Further contributions to the theory and technique of Psycho-analysis*. (pp. 105–109). UK: Karnac Books, 1994.

―――― (1930). The principles of relaxation and neocatharsis. In *Final contributions to the problems and methods of psycho–analysis*. (pp. 108–125). UK: Karnac Books, 1994. Also in *International Journal of Psychoanalysis*, 11, 428–443. 1930.

―――― (1932). *The Clinical Diary of Sándor Ferenczi*. J. Dupont (Ed.), M. Balint & N.Z. Jackson (Trans.). Cambridge, MA. & London: Harvard University Press, 1988.

―――― (1933). Confusion of tongues between adults and the child. The language of tenderness and of passion. In *Final contribution to the problems and methods of Psycho–analysis*. (pp. 156–167). UK: Karnac Books, 1994. Also, in *International Journal of Psychoanalysis*, 30, 225–230, 1949.

Freud, A. (1936). *The ego and the mechanisms of defence*. London: Hogarth Press.

Freud, S., & Ferenczi, S. (1908–1914). *The correspondence of Sigmund Freud and Sándor Ferenczi, Volume 1. 1908–1914*. E. Brabant, E. Falzeder & P. Giampieri-Deutsch (Eds.), P. T. Hoffer (Trans.). With an Introduction by and under the supervision of A. Haynal. Cambridge, MA & London: The Belknap Press of Harvard University Press, 1992.

————— & Ferenczi, S. (1914–1919). *The correspondence of Sigmund Freud and Sándor Ferenczi, Volume 2. 1914–1919.* E. Falzeder & E. Brabant, (Eds.), P. T. Hoffer (Trans.), under the supervision of A. Haynal. With an Introduction by A. Hoffer. Cambridge, MA& London: The Belknap Press of Harvard University Press, 1996.

————— & ————— (1920–1933). *The correspondence of Sigmund Freud and Sándor Ferenczi, Volume 3. 1920–1933.* E. Falzeder & E. Brabant (Eds.), with the collaboration of P. Giampieri-Deutsch under the supervision of A. Haynal, P. T. Hoffer (Trans.). With an Introduction by J. Dupont. Cambridge, Mass & London: The Belknap Press of Harvard University Press, 2000.

Fromm, E. (1963). Psychoanalysis—Science or party line? In *The Dogma of Christ.* New York: Holt, Rinehart and Winston, pp. 131–144.

Galdi, G. (1998) (Ed.). Introduction to the Special Issue: The contributions of Sándor Ferenczi. *American Journal of Psychoanalysis, 58,* 1–4.

Hoffer, A. (1991). The Freud–Ferenczi controversy—A living legacy. *International Review of Psycho-Analysis, 18,* 465–472.

Rudnytsky, P. (1991). *The psychoanalytic vocation: Rank, Winnicott, and the legacy of Freud.* New Haven, CT: Yale University Press.

Response to Dr. Giselle Galdi

Carolyn Ellman

I am very grateful to Dr. Galdi for her very careful reading of my paper "The Power of Exclusion". I agree with her that everyone should read the three-volume correspondence between Freud and Ferenczi to clarify some of the misunderstandings about their relationship and his involvement with Elma. It was that correspondence that sparked my interest in writing this paper. I would also like to thank her for clarifying the list of patients (I am adding Vilma Kovacs and Theresa Benedek) and omitting Mahler, Spitz and Rank. Since Freud said in his obituary about Ferenczi that he was the "analyst to all analysts" it did seem sometimes as if everyone at that time was sent to Ferenczi.

I would also like to comment on the omission of Ferenczi from the list of presidents of the International Psychoanalytic Association since I find his omission from many discussions is an on-going problem. Since I first presented this paper to a Contemporary Freudian Institute, I found many colleagues had never read Ferenczi. Many of them proceeded to read the *Clinical Diaries* and were very appreciative of the brilliance of that work. However, I still find myself the only one that brings him up at various scientific meetings. The damage has been done.

I also appreciate that she quoted from the *Diary* entry of October 2nd, 1932. I remember when I first read it and how painful it was. It is very important to read the inner struggle he was going through in his attachment to Freud to understand the depths of some of these issues that he felt he had to stand up for against very deep despair about not being understood.

As a final comment, I was also glad to read that Balint told Winnicott how often his ideas were similar to Ferenczi's since while I was reading the *Clinical Dairies* the similarities were so striking.

Most of all, I am so grateful to have a true Ferenczi scholar read my work since as a Contemporary Freudian I came to Ferenczi very late and yet truly fell in love with him. I thank Dr. Galdi for taking the time to read this paper and comment on it.

———

Brief note on Ellman-Galdi discussions

M. Sagman Kayatekin

Ellman and Galdi's contributions in this volume made me think about the subject of writing history that increasingly is becoming a focus of interest of mine.

There seems to be a subtle shift in writing the history of persons, thought collectives or social issues from a different lens. A central element in this style of writing, to my understanding, is the fact that it goes beyond being a documentation of the development of important, novel ideas or social changes in a vacuum. The stance includes other human elements that partly initiate or shape these controversies. Intellectual, political climate of the times, individual predilections, group dynamics of ordinary daily life that center around jealousy, allegiances, attachments etc. Half a century ego Brian Bird was making an oblique reference to some aspects of this phenomenon as transference being a most important ego function that also shapes creativity. (Bird 1972)

The other central element of this stance is, the history is written from the moment it was happening, rather than history as a retrospectively constructed, linear, inevitable development to our moment where we have the ultimate, developed theory or whatever is under scrutiny. Thus, added to our customary approaches like determinism, relatively unexamined paradigms, such as the role of randomness, chance, will, decisions, choices, and creativity enter the picture.

From my personal interest on processes and periods of personal or social change, two examples that fit this style of history writing are the works of Avineri and Gewarth, both from our neighboring disciplines in social sciences (Avineri 2019, Gewarth 2020).

In sum, it is a multifaceted history that is worked out laboriously and meticulously. A history devoid of simple causes, teleological linear developments, simple generalities. Quite similar to what we aim to achieve in our daily psychoanalytic work, one may say.

References

Avineri S. *Karl Marx: Philosophy and Revolution. Jewish Lives.* Edited by Anita Shapira and Steven J. Zipperstein. New Haven, CT: Yale University Press, 2019.

Bird, B. Notes on Transference: Universal Phenomenon and Hardest Part of Analysis. *Journal of the American Psychoanalytic Association* 20:267–301, 1972.

Gerwarth R. *November 1918: The German Revolution.* (Making of the Modern World series). Oxford: Oxford University Press, 2020.

About the Contributors

Daniel S. Benveniste, PhD, is a clinical psychologist with a private practice in Sammamish, Washington, near Seattle. He is a Visiting Professor of Clinical Psychology at the Wuhan Mental Health Center, in the People's Republic of China and an Honorary Member of the American Psychoanalytic Association. He is the author of *Libido, Culture, and Consciousness: Revisiting Freud's Totem and Taboo* (2022), *The Interwoven Lives of Sigmund, Anna, and W. Ernest Freud: Three Generations of Psychoanalysis* (2015) and *The Venezuelan Revolution: A Critique from the Left* (2015). He is also the editor of *Anna Freud in the Hampstead Clinic: Letters to Humberto Nágera* (2015) and edited *IJCD: International Journal of Controversial Discussions,* Volume 3, Issue One.

He earned his BA (1976), MS (1979) and PhD (1990) in clinical psychology in the San Francisco Bay Area and was in supervision with Nathan Adler, Ph.D., for five years. He began his private practice and teaching career in San Francisco. From 1999 to 2010, he lived and worked in Caracas, Venezuela, where he maintained a private practice and taught psychotherapy at two universities. In 2010 he relocated to the Pacific Northwest with his wife, Adriana Prengler, FIPA.

Christina Biedermann, PsyD, ABAP, is an Associate Professor at the Illinois School of Professional Psychology at National Louis University as well as a practicing clinical psychologist and psychoanalyst. She is also Clinical Associate Faculty at the Chicago Center for

Psychoanalysis and an Associate Editor for the Book Review of the *Journal of the American Psychoanalytic Association.* In addition, she reviews for *Psychoanalytic Psychology* and the *Journal of Feminist Family Therapy* and has presented at national conferences on menopause, working with complex trauma, suicidality, treatment resistance, psychological assessment, and feminist advocacy, as well as lectured at the Yale Child Study Center, the Yale-Riggs Family and Infant Mental Health training program, and the New York Psychoanalytic Society and Institute.

Her current academic interests include: reproductive psychology and justice, motherhood and maternal subjectivity, women's mental health, complex trauma, psychodynamic theory and psychotherapy, and education and training in psychodynamic psychology.

Thomas DePrima, MD, is a psychiatrist and psychoanalyst in practice in Manhattan. He received his AB in Biology at Harvard University and then his MD from the University of Miami Miller School of Medicine. He completed his adult psychiatry residency at Mount Sinai and completed psychoanalytic training at New York Psychoanalytic Society & Institute. He continues to be a member at NYPSI serving on the faculty and on various committees. He is currently the associate medical director of the World Trade Center Mental Health Program at Mount Sinai, a program set up by the Federal Government to treat 9/11 responders who would go on to develop medical issues as a consequence of their rescue and recovery work. Earlier in his life, he was an accomplished percussionist. He performed in 35 countries as a member of the Long Island Youth Orchestra, an organization that he now serves as Vice President of the Board of Directors. He also performed in musical segments on two episodes of Sesame Street as a child in 1997.

Carolyn Ellman, PhD, Graduate of the NYU Postdoctoral Program in Psychoanalysis and Psychotherapy. Fellow and Faculty-Institute for Psychoanalytic Training and Research (IPTAR) Adjunct Clinical Professor and Supervisor NYU. Postdoctoral Program in Psychotherapy and Psychoanalysis; Training and Supervising Analyst Contemporary Freudian Society; Member of IPA and CIPS; Senior Editor of *The Modern Freudians: Contemporary Psychoanalytic Technique* by Jason Aronson in 2000 and *Omnipotent Fantasies and the Vulnerable.* Self published by Jason Aronson in 1997; Co-Editor *A New Freudian Synthesis: Clinical Process in a new generation* by Karnac Books 2011 (with Andrew Druck, Norbert Freedman and Aaron Thaler). Author of many articles on Envy in women. Recipient of the Doris Bernstein Memorial Lecture IPTAR, Honorary Fingert Lecture St. Louis Psychoanalytic Institute and the Norbert Freedman Memorial Lecture at IPTAR. In private practice in New York.

Giselle Galdi, PhD was the Editor of the *American Journal of Psychoanalysis* for 25 years, one of the oldest psychoanalytic journals in the US, founded by Karen Horney in 1941. The *AJP* is celebrating its 85th year of continuous publication in 2025, the year Giselle stepped down as Editor in Chief. During her editorship the *AJP* published many Special Issues and articles, dedicated to Ferenczi's legacy.

She is Training and Supervising Analyst and former Director of Training at the American Institute for Psychoanalysis, which was established in 1941 by Karen Horney, and is the second oldest training institute in the New York Metropolitan area. She was also the Director of

171

the Trauma Treatment Center of the renowned Karen Horney Clinic for many years.

An important aspect of Giselle's work is her 35–year involvement with the Ferenczi revival. She introduced the formal teaching of Ferenczi into the curriculum of the American Institute for Psychoanalysis in 1995 and taught the course for many years. Giselle is on the Board of Directors of the Sándor Ferenczi Center of the New School in NYC, she is a Program Committee Member of the International Sándor Ferenczi Conferences and is on the Board of Directors of the International Sándor Ferenczi Network (ISFN). (https://www.sandorferenczi.org).

The next International Sándor Ferenczi Conference will be held in Madrid from October 14 to 17, 2026. (https://www.sandorferenczi.org/conferences/ next-international-ferenczi-conference/).

She is also one of the editors of the recently announced project of the ISFN to issue an updated edition of Ferenczi's works, "The Network Edition of the Writings of Sándor Ferenczi."

Dr. Galdi is in private practice in New York City.

M. Sagman Kayatekin, MD, graduated from Hacettepe University Medical Faculty and completed residency trainings in adult psychiatry at Hacettepe and Medical College of Wisconsin. He had a four-year fellowship at the Austen Riggs Center and graduated from Boston Psychoanalytic Society and Institute as an adult psychoanalyst. He was faculty at Hacettepe, UMass, and Baylor. He is currently faculty and former President of the Board at Center for Psychoanalytic Studies, Visiting Professor at Tongji Medical College, China. He also has faculty position at Psychoanalytic Institute for Central Asia, Kazakhstan. In the last 40 years, he maintained a dual interest in clinical care and teaching while directing various

clinical organizations. He taught, published and presented in a wide range of national and international forums. His most recent role was as the Medical Director of Professionals Program at the Menninger Clinic. All through these years he also had a small private practice on the sides. Since 2022, he mainly works in his private practice and is involved in clinical work, teaching, lecturing, writing and supervision. Some of his current areas of interest are pedagogy of psychoanalytic training, ego capacities of the mind, the central role of language in understanding the mind, and the controversial/creative subjects in psychoanalytic theory and practice.

Merle Molofsky, MFA, NCPsyA, is a New York State-licensed psychoanalyst in private practice. She is a member of the Editorial Board of *The Psychoanalytic Review,* of the Editorial Board of *The International Journal of Controversial Discussions,* and of the Advisory Council of the Harlem Family Institute (HFI). Her play, Kool-Aid, was produced at Lincoln Center. Her publications include a novel, *Streets 1970;* a collection of short fiction, *Necessary Voices;* a collection of poetry, *Sh'ma, I Hear Voices;* and an edited book, *Jew Hating: The Black Milk of Civilization,* all published by IPBooks. She also has contributed chapters to several psychoanalytic books, has published several other collections of her poetry, and numerous articles. She received the Gradiva Award in Poetry in 2012 from the National Association for the Advancement of Psychoanalysis (NAAP). In the past, she served as Dean of Training at NPAP, as Director of Education at the Institute for Expressive Analysis (IEA), and as Editor of the online psychoanalytic journal *Other/Wise.* She received her psychoanalytic education at NPAP, and has served on the faculties of the Training Institute of NPAP, the Institute for Expressive Analysis (IEA), and the Harlem Family Institute (HFI).

Adriana Prengler, originally from Buenos Aires, Argentina, is a clinical psychologist who trained at the Caracas Psychoanalytic Society in Venezuela and later emigrated to the United States (Seattle) in 2010. She is a training and supervising analyst at the Northwestern Psychoanalytic Society and Institute (NPSI) and at the Caracas Psychoanalytic Society (SCP). She is a Visiting Professor of Clinical Psychology at the Wuhan Mental Health Center, in China.

She has published articles in English and Spanish on immigration, identification, loss, mourning and the influence of cultural differences on the psyche. She has presented these ideas in adult and child clinical case presentations, and film interpretations.

She served as vice-president of the International Psychoanalytical Association from 2021–2025 and many other positions in FEPAL and the IPA including founding Chair of the IPA Candidates' Loan Panel, the IPA Psychoanalysts' Emigration and Relocation Committee (PERC) and she created the IPA Committee for Psychoanalysts assistance in Crisis and Emergencies (PACE).

She maintains a private practice with adults, couples, adolescents and children in Sammamish, Washington, near Seattle.

Arlene Kramer Richards, EdD, is a psychoanalyst and a poet. She is a Training and Supervising Analyst with the Contemporary Freudian Society and the International Psychoanalytic Association and Fellow of IPTAR. She is currently faculty at the CFS and Tongji Medical College of Huazhong University of Science and Technology at Wuhan, China. Her education at the University of Chicago introduced her to the dialogues of Plato.

That gave her a sense of what she now thinks of as her calling. Talking with people who are willing to learn her truth and teach her theirs has been the theme of her professional life. Psychoanalysis gave her her voice and focused her listening. It made excellent use of her curiosity and her love for teaching others. She especially enjoy conversations with ancient authors, feeling like a time traveler in conversation with the past.

www.ingramcontent.com/pod-product-compliance
Lightning Source LLC
Chambersburg PA
CBHW060227030426
42335CB00014B/1360